Arcs of Mind:
Theory of the Literary Creative Cycle

By

Wendell Jackson

To my wonderful wife, Edith, who afforded me the leisure and support to complete this project.

Contents

Man puts things in a row.
Things belong in a row.
The showing of the true row is science.[1]
– Ralph Waldo Emerson

It is a truth perpetually, that accumulated facts, lying in disorder, begin to assume some order if an hypothesis is thrown among them.[2]
– Herbert Spencer

---

[1] Emerson and Gilman (5: 168)
[2] Spencer (136)

PART ONE: THE WRITER'S EARLIEST OR PRE-CREATIVE THOUGHT PROCESSES

The notion that there is a literary creative process which triggers in the would-be writer certain mental arcs or intellectual trajectories is intriguing in the extreme. If there is such a process, it certainly is loathe to reveal itself, and all we can do is develop a probable outline or theory. In doing so, we must acknowledge certain boundaries, which are that: 1. we have before us psychology or philosophy, but not science; 2. we have to cognize certain processes which are both interior and exterior to the writer; 3. we must admit the arbitrariness or relativity of what we are attempting; 4. we must acknowledge the source of our evidence; 5. we must explain why this effort is beneficial; and 6. we must offer a preview of what we think we see.

1. <u>The Book's Inscriptions and the Disclaimer as to Science</u>. May we say at the outset that, though charmingly stated and philosophically suggestive, the book's inscriptions should not lead us to think that anything to be discussed here is "science" in the usual sense of the word – that is, the notion of being based upon demonstrable fact and of being predictive. But these inscriptions do reverberate in our minds when we think of the idea of patterns, of generalizations, and of hypotheses which, though not science, are nonetheless useful and informative guides, in the same way that we speak of psychological or philosophical guidelines and generalizations.

In this effort, the stages or phases of a creative process will not necessarily or always be sequential, as presented here for the sake of description. These so-called stages will almost certainly be simultaneous and intertwined in expressing themselves. It would be misleading to think otherwise. But as a theoretical enterprise, this sequential and even seemingly mechanical description is both necessary and interesting. This study is an attempt to describe creative processes which seem to come into play in the production of literature; and the project is prompted by the fact that over the years, examination of the literary creative process has been, not only inadequate (in relation to the study of creativity in general and of literary creativity in particular), but also seemingly uncoordinated.

With respect to the question of adequacy, six main types of sources suggest themselves when we discuss creativity in general (although there will certainly be others): a. philosophical discussions of the nature of creativity;[3] b. clinical assessments of genius or explanations of the psychology of creativity;[4] c. scholarly studies of the function and limits of literature and of the arts;[5] d. observations or generalizations about the creative experience, from creative individuals themselves;[6] e. detailed case studies of particular writers or of other creative individuals;[7] and f. a few comprehensive bibliographies concerning creativity

---

3. These, of course, would be very general works like Kant's *Critique of Judgment*, Maritain's *Creative Intuition in Art and Poetry*, or Sartre's *What Is Literature*.

4 This type of study is obviously a branch of psychology.

5 Wellek and Warren's *Theory of Literature* is a good example of this type of source.

6 These include such anthologies or collections as Ghiselin 's *The Creative Process: A Symposium*; Plimpton and Oates's *The Paris Review Interviews: Writers at Work*; and Rothenberg and Houseman's *The Creativity Question*.

7 Many literary or critical studies seem to fall into this category.

across many fields.[8] Of these six sources, the overwhelming amount of work has been either critical assessment of individual literary or artistic pieces or the study of the clinical dimensions of genius or creativity. But these same six sources suggest the dearth of descriptions of a literary creative cycle as a synthetic whole; for, with regard to the question of coordination, it is obvious that few (if any) of the studies that do examine the literary creative process have emphasized the synthetic or whole "life cycle" of a work; they rather have focused upon specific aspects of literary creation. These studies have left largely unaddressed the question of what constitutes the overall "life" of literature -- the creative processes by which literature comes to be, by which it is sustained or preserved, and even by which it undergoes a process of demise and later of regeneration. It is widely-acknowledged, however, that, in due course, a literary work does undergo some peculiar cycle, though there necessarily is a divergence of opinion as to the elements of such a cycle.

2. **Nature of This Project**. Despite what may appear to be obvious, this is also not a cook book on how to write a poem or story. Rather, it is an effort to describe the functioning of the writer's mind as it follows the trajectory from personal challenges, to the moment of inspiration, to the conversion of this inspiration into a creative idea, to the use of this idea to produce a literary object, to the finale of dispensing this object to a given culture; and to the cultural use of this product of the writer's mind. In all of these stages, directly or indirectly, the creative contribution of the individual writer must be involved or

---

8 A useful example is Arestah's *Creativity in the Life Cycle: An Annotated Bibliography*.

implied. Hence, this examination points unavoidably to the writer as the guiding or at least delimiting factor in the entire creative process. One realizes that reference to the writer as the guiding factor in the creation of literature takes a step away from some more recent emphases upon the work as an object unrelated to the consciousness of the writer. In some sense, there is reason to acknowledge the validity of this point of view as expressed by reader-response or reader-reception criticism, although this approach seems most valid after the work is sent out to the public. At that point, admittedly, the work is an object that must speak wholly for itself or not at all. But disassociating the work (if that is the theory) totally from the consciousness or influence of the writer (even for the purpose of critiquing it) seems a real distortion!

It appears, even further, that any act of creativity is by its nature an interactive process, beginning, it may be, as an impulse of the individual writer, but ending invariably (or at least inferentially) as an impact upon some group of readers, upon whom the writer seeks to make an impression. We also must add the somewhat sobering thought that this interactive process is just as routinely and powerfully reversed, involving a possibly reciprocal impulse or impact from the group of readers that can end in influencing writers. One has to ask whether the literary process can be fully understood without this assumed reciprocity?

3. Relativity of Our Construct. We do not in any way assert that the construct built here is definitive, and we acknowledge that a different researcher could and probably would derive a construct that is quite different. Rather, our goal is to see what kind of construct is possible if we attempted to connect the

6

stubborn dots or to draw connecting lines, in an effort to arrive at a plausible and unifying picture. The concepts here must stand on their own as mere suggestions of a possible or even probable mental process, and (as we have stated) it is freely acknowledged that other formulations may be just as probable or even desirable. It must also be noted that this whole enterprise reflects this writer's own groping (mostly blindly), as he grapples with the difficult and puzzling concept of the creative endeavor. Our blundering repetitions and speculations are a symptom of the struggle to understand, to assemble, and partially to explain what it is we can only minimally perceive.

4. **Emersonian Source**. In this particular discussion, we are exploring literary creative processes through the journals of Ralph Waldo Emerson, because Emerson, over many decades, had done a good bit of spontaneous thinking and offered many raw insights into the creation of literature. Accordingly, we have sought to fit together bits and pieces of perception from his journals, to form the outlines of a whole, though this whole may be found to be independent of Emerson's own intellectual synthesis of this material or his lack of synthesis, especially since Emerson's somewhat unsuccessful attempt at synthesis is recorded for us even in his essays, which reveal his struggle to organize his thoughts. In other words, what we are trying to do here may not truthfully be called Emersonian, in that, though Emerson's perceptions constitute the data from which we draw, Emerson may or may not have endorsed the arrangement of these perceptions into the picture which we are attempting to present.

5. <u>Benefits</u>. Examination of this supposed "life cycle" would seem to offer many benefits to those who attempt to understand some of the possible parameters of literary creation, and who wish, eventually, to raise an even deeper question about processes in the life of literature -- namely, the question of whether or not discernible phases in the literary cycle are part of an underlying (and unavoidable) "blueprint" or "template" which human beings are constrained to follow if they are to bring forth any literary work (and for that matter, any creative production)!

6. <u>Elements of the Perceived Pattern</u>. On the one hand, we might say that intellectual patterns, if they do exist, consist of three, self-evident phases – a pre-creative stage (involving questions personally touching the writer such as opportunity and inclination), a central or creative phase (concerning the subject matter and formation of a work), and a post-creative period (involving the cultural appropriation and use of the work).

Seen through an alternate and more specific lens, the observer might also distinguish seven states, stages, or sequential or overlapping movements:

a. A totally preliminary mind set, in which conscious creative production is admitted as even possible, a stage that is exemplified by the assertions of this very introductory chapter;

b. A preparatory process, in which the readiness of the individual writer is evidenced;

c. A procedure by which the creative spark is ignited or in which the literary idea is first sensed by the writer;

d. One in which this creative spark grows into a tangible literary form or is made creatively concrete by the writer;

e. One in which the writer sends the completed work out to the public;

f. One in which the received work makes its cultural impact, thereby completing the (for Emerson) obvious goal of the creative effort itself, namely, that of influencing readers; and

g. One in which the critical response of readers to a particular work can add to the literary canon, can help writers produce something new, and can thus suggest the overall cyclical nature of the literary creative process itself.

Hopefully, these speculations as to patterns will encourage others to formulate their own hypotheses.

Speaking of the first or Pre-Creative Phase of the writer's thinking, we cannot help observing that a critical key to the success of the creative process is resolution of an inexorable mental conflict – that between personal forces which may detract from the achievement of the writer and those which augment or enhance the writer's success. It is almost as though writing is not a "natural" state, if by the term "natural" we mean the common or inertial condition which emphasizes the personal survival of writers, as opposed to the flowering or implementation of their visions, dreams, or artistic objectives. The mundane necessity required for survival must pull them in one direction; and their ambitions as writers, in another. In this conflict (this seeming war), health, commitment, and leisure appear to be the trophies over which the battles are fought. Were writers not to struggle against many hindering circumstances, they would experience only delay and shattered aims. To be in a position to produce literary work, therefore, writers have consciously to preserve their vitality or physical health; display exceptional commitment; and accrue to themselves a considerable amount of leisure, out of which alone creative thought can be generated.

1.<u>Vitality</u>. For serious productivity, writers must acknowledge their need for a significant degree of physical vitality or health, throughout their career. This vitality renders them competent to perform the needed work: "But beside the strange power implied of passing at will into the state of vision and of utterance, is

11

required huge means, vast health and vigor and celerity" [Emerson and Emerson (viii: 540-541)]. If endowed "with a cheerful, happy temper, and well-adjusted to the tone of the human race," then they can feel "in the harmony of things, and conscious of an infinite strength," a superabundance which leads, in turn, to action or productivity, enabling them to "build a railroad, make a fortune, write an Iliad," as a compensation to themselves for their abnormally vitalized position [Emerson and Emerson (vii: 246)]. With this abundance, the writer can "[subjugate] ... matter to be the servant, the instrument of thought and heart," rather than allowing "a particle of matter ... [to obstruct] and defeat ...." [Emerson and Emerson (ix: 298)] When this subjugation occurs, matter becomes "opulence, and light, and beauty and joy" [Emerson and Emerson (ix: 298)]. A related issue grows from Emerson's observation, "What is good to make me happy is not however good to make me write" [Emerson and Emerson (v: 292)], by means of which comment he draws a clear distinction between the personality of the individual and the entity which is the inner, creative self.

Where writers are not born with this abundance, they have to husband what they have. Of this idea of making the best of one's physical limitations or health, Emerson himself is an excellent example. He bitterly laments his "lameness" of organ. When he is ill, he complains, "the thought I would utter to my friend comes forth in stony, sepulchral tones, I am disgusted, and I will not speak more.... A puny, limitary creature am I, with only a small annuity of vital force to expend, which if I squander in a few feast days, I must feed on water and moss the rest of the time" [Emerson and Emerson (v: 516)]. Should Emerson attempt to compensate for this deficiency by overextending himself, he is ruined for the next project and retreats to the miserly practice of spending himself "prudently" -- only to find that nothing grand ever grows from penury [Emerson and Emerson (vii: 176; v: 246-247)], from "lassitude," except mediocrity [Emerson and Emerson (x: 42)]. Acquiescing at last to the thought that his Genius is "stingy," leaving him "faint and sprawling" when he extends himself beyond his meager, daily apportionment of energy, Emerson admits to having arrived at "a perfect selfishness," having grown "circumspect and disobliging beyond the example of all the misers" [Emerson and Emerson (vii: 37)]. Even when writers are endowed with great vitality or have learned, like Emerson, to function at a level of lowered vitality, they encounter one of the keenest ironies of life: that, by the time they acquire "as much skill in literature as an old carpenter does in wood," their organs fail; in fact, their "eyes, health, fire, and zeal of work ..." are decaying daily [Emerson and Emerson (viii: 303 - 304)], so that, under this creeping decay, "only in rare moments, and by happiest combination or consent of the elements, can they attain those enlargements and that intellectual elan," which either once were "a daily gift" [Emerson and Emerson (x: 47)] or an aim to which they daily aspired.

Emerson concludes that, since writing is primarily an interior activity, writers need "a frolick health to execute" their work, if they are ever to be productive [Emerson and Emerson (vii: 190)]; for, stated differently, writing cannot unfold in a vacuum unrelated to the vitality which flows through authors into their creation. Without this personal, physical fire, they can take not even the first step towards credible artistic production.

2. <u>Commitment</u>. Not only must writers possess adequate health or vitality, but beyond that possession, they must express

an extraordinary sense of mission, endure much sacrifice, and evidence a keen efficiency. One bit of evidence that they experience a keen sense of that mission is their peculiar consciousness of "a great work" to complete and a belief that Nature "cannot afford" to lose them until that work is finished [Emerson and Emerson (ix: 191 - 92)]. Trusting the future more than the past and present, they hear "voices" calling them to their task [Emerson and Emerson (vii: 173)]

Unavoidably, then, "the artist is in some degree sacrificed" to his work [Emerson and Emerson (vi: 82 - 83)]. That is another way of saying that to their work writers must give all or nothing, must subordinate life to this inner purpose. The "writer must live and die by his writing. Good for that, and good for nothing else. A war, an earthquake, the revival of letters, and new dispensation by Jesus, or by Angels, Heaven, Hell, Power, Science, the Neant, exist only to him as colors for his brush." Those who think that authors can do less, "can write at odd minutes," reveal their ignorance [Emerson and Emerson (vii: 187)].

This devotion, which keeps "the old man constant to the same pursuits as in youth," resembles "the diurnal, annual, and centennial variations of the magnet." The "force of the spring which we call native bias or character" gives us "that incessant nudge to necessity or of passion to drive us from idleness and bring the day about...." [Emerson and Emerson (ix: 539)] What makes most people "sketches," rather than "finished" human beings, Emerson asserts, is that they have not yet found this "native bias" [Emerson and Emerson (ix: 577)], which gives them the power to create "value": Everyone "was created to augment some real value, and not for a speculator." When an individual "leaves or postpones (as most … do) [their] proper work, and adopts some short or cunning method, as of watching markets, or farming in any

14

manner the ignorance of people, as, in buying by the acre to sell by the foot," they are "fraudulent," they are "malefactor[s], so far" and are "bringing society to bankruptcy" [Emerson and Emerson (ix: 527)].

Since the "muse demands real sacrifices" of this kind, the writer cannot, simultaneously, "be a poet and a paterfamilias and a militia captain" [Emerson and Emerson (vii: 173)]; for though the work of a mechanic ends at night, that of the scholar is unending [Emerson and Emerson (vii: 107)]. Indeed, the "poetic experiences" of writers cost them much time [Emerson and Emerson (x: 69-70)]. If they can experience such dedication, they can avoid sacrificing their higher objectives to goals which are secondary, transitory, even trivial: "We meant well, but our uncle was crazy and must be restrained from waking the house. The roof leaked, we were out of wood ...; there were taxes to pay, and notes, and, alas, a tomb to build: we were obliged continually to postpone our best action, and that which was life to do could only be smuggled into odd moments of the month and year" [Emerson and Emerson (viii: 520 - 21)].

3. <u>Leisure</u>. In addition to vitality and commitment, writers need leisure (or time) in which to conceive and execute their plans – time which they can obtain by finding financial support, by being released honorably from society's routines and reforms, and by removing themselves from other avoidable distractions.

Writers deserve the financial support of the community. The right of writers to financial support comes from their ability, through their powers of communication, "to direct the means of the community, to select and aid and enrich the youth of genius and virtue" [Emerson and Emerson (v: 337-338)]. Even merchants know in their heart that this work is necessary and the reason for which they have done all of their trading: so that their daughter or son may benefit from the fruits of culture, partly embodied in the writer's communication. For this reason, Emerson abhors "[t]his atheism of the priest, this prose of the poet, this cowardice and succumbing before material greatness," calling it "a treason one knows not how to excuse" [Emerson and Emerson (viii: 471 - 73)]. That is to say, scholars and artists must exhibit a sense of proportion when dealing with people of status and wealth and beware otherwise "courting" the frivolous [Emerson and Emerson viii: 485 - 86)]. For this same reason, poets should be wary of both power and fame; for they are least poets "when they sit crowned. The transcendental and divine has [sic] the dominion of the world on the sole condition of not having it" [Emerson and Emerson vii: 198)]. Stated differently, Emerson abhors any tendency of writers "to talk and sit with the rich" and thereby "sympathize with them" [Emerson and Emerson viii: 466-67)] For Emerson, the college and its resultant arts and sciences are "not to make you rich or great, but to show you that material pomps and possessions, that all feats of our civility, were first the thoughts of good heads" and that "All powers by which [one] lays [one's] hand on these advantages are intellectual; it is thoughts that make [us] great and strong; the material results are bubbles, filled only and coloured by this divine air."[9] Thus, it is up to scholars to show the people that "intellect is the thread on which all their worldly prosperity is strung." In fact, Emerson again asserts, the more important value of the arts and sciences, of poetry and thought, is not their "secular and outward benefit"; rather, "[a]ll that is urged by the saint for the superiority of faith over works is as truly urged for

---

[9] As we shall see in the next chapter, this notion that practically all that is creative in culture derives from a few thinkers is the foundation of Emerson's theory as to the origin of subject matter in writing.

16

the highest state of intellectual perception over any performance." Though Emerson insists that he values "practical ability," delights "in people who can do things," and prizes worldly talent more than anyone else, he thinks "of the wind, and not of the weathercocks" [Emerson and Emerson (viii: 471 - 73)].

However, if the public attitude is that artists cost too much [Emerson and Emerson (vii: 176)], then society should not chastise them for selling their wisdom, to prevent themselves from being put in a "most awkward relation to loaves of bread" [Emerson and Emerson (viii: 428)]. If they did not sell their books under these circumstances, they would have to "desert ... their function in the commonwealth, untimely deny themselves and those whom they ought to serve the first means of education." And if they forsake these duties, it will be "to the detriment of all learning and civility...." [Emerson and Emerson (v: 337-38)]; for society should remember that "all the expenditures of a truly cultivated" individual are "like the expenditures of a temple, religious and public" [Emerson and Emerson (viii: 485 - 86)]. Thus, society must "leave open to them the resource of selling the works, which are the only vendible product of so many laborious days and watching nights, and whose price ought to be esteemed sacred, and not vile" [Emerson and Emerson (v:337 - 38)].

Further, for the very reason that writers' lives are interior, not external; because we know them, not by their biography but by the "catalogue" of their works [Emerson and Emerson (v: 265)], they cannot rise to society's expectation that they be practical reformers [Emerson and Emerson (vii: 267)]. Rather, since literature is a gamble, writers "should be delivered as much as may be from societal routine, to increase" their chances [Emerson and Emerson (vi: 467)]. Yet, through many avenues, society "sucks" writers' "vitals into some one or other bitter partiality," thereby depriving them of that condition of "adequateness" for which they pray [Emerson and Emerson (vii: 209)]. In fact, judging from his own experience (and despite, he again acknowledges, all the "fine things" he has said about the manual labor of literary people), Emerson wonders whether writers (for whom "the grasshopper is a burden") "ought to be released from every species of public or private responsibility," which "untune[s] and disquali[fies]" them for writing.[10] For the reason that writers must have leisure, Emerson even, therefore, appreciates the Roman Catholic position on monastic life, including the celibacy of its clergy [Emerson and Emerson (v: 517 - 18)].

Since there are so many other spirits in the world, cannot writers be "spared" to finish their chapters in such a way that they and others can read them without pain [Emerson and Emerson (x: 269 - 270)]? Nor would this prudent release from added responsibility provoke criticism, in that" [i]f you are abandoned to your genius and employment, be it never so special and rare,...[people] will do you justice and not reproach you that you do not plough" [Emerson and Emerson (vii: 141)]. In fact, "[c]alm, pure, effectual service distinguishes the generous soul from the vulgar great" [Emerson and Emerson (vi: 521)]. What matters, then, is not whether people "devote themselves to nouns or to laying stone walls, but whether they do it honestly or for show" [Emerson and Emerson (vi: 521)].

Because, Emerson complains, what "untunes" him "is as bad as what cripples or stuns," writers would do well to place themselves away from the boisterous and worrisome claims of

---

[10] We might consider Emerson's largely skeptical attitude towards the Brook Farm experiment (1841 - 1847). This idealistic, even utopian, commune was founded in Massachusetts in part by George and Sophia Ripley. Its leading concept was that of shared, usually manual labor, and shared profit or benefits.

daily living. Only then can they achieve the required mental poise [Emerson and Emerson (x: 43 - 44)] and the right conditions for the needed work. It is futile, therefore, to ask poets "to come to the aid of the disturbed institutions." The poet should reply: "'I can best help by going on with the creation of my own. I am a sad bungler at laws, being afflicted with a certain inconsecutiveness of thought, impertinent association, and extreme skepticism; but I recover my eyesight and spirit in solitude'" [Emerson and Emerson (vii: 175)]. Because in their work they invest their time, they cannot, therefore, give you this same time: they must give you that into which they put their time: a letter, poem, or opinion [Emerson and Emerson (v: 471)]. Emerson quotes from Vasari's[11] *Life of Fra Angelico* on the need for solitude; for "'He who practices the art of painting had need of quiet, and should live without cares or anxious thoughts'" [Emerson and Emerson (viii: 211)]. The advantage of solitude is that it allows the thinker to pursue a few ideas as though they were "the gods of his Temple," sufficing him "for intellect and heart for years." Because of this concentration, "[t]he solitary worshiper knows the essence of the thought," whereas "the scholar in society sees only its fair face" [Emerson and Emerson (x: 65-66)]. Sadly, by virtue of this required solitude, writers isolate themselves from society; and society, conversely, isolates itself from them. The "sweet opium" which they have "learned to chew" and which they call "Muses, and Memory, and philosophy," sometimes allows them to feel justified in their mysterious and solitary activity because of the "perfect sympathy" they find when they meet other writers and scholars. But in the meantime, society leaves them more and

---

[11] Vasari, Giorgio (1511 -- 1574). Painter, writer, and historian of the Italian Renaissance. The Fra Angelico referred to lived from 1395 – 1455, and the quality of his painting is praised in Vasari's *Lives of the Artists*.

more out of its affairs; and their "faculties languish for want of invitation, and objective work," until they become the very self-indulgent dreamers society taunts them with being [Emerson and Emerson (viii: 387)].[12]

Emerson not only emphasizes the need of health or vitality and makes suggestions which may enhance this need, but also he speaks of the necessity of a one-pointed mission, a determination that writers pursue their ideas, even to the point of great personal sacrifice. Alongside these two qualities of vitality and commitment, he addresses the need for leisure. In certain respects, it is misleading to call the last part of Emerson's discussion, "leisure," for leisure is not an end but a means. Leisure, as the nexus in which effective thought can occur, is the doorway to the whole issue of inspiration, which is the next question concerning the mind of the writer which we must consider.

---

[12] As definite as these convictions may have seemed to Emerson when he voiced them, there is ample evidence to suggest that he came to modify these views. Indeed, over time Emerson "turned from being an intellectual and social recluse," to assuming the role of a devoted social reformer. Even so, many of his assertions about leisure appear justified (See Jackson, "Burden").

The Second, Central, or Creative, Phase of the life of literature is obviously a more subjective one, because this creative activity naturally takes us further into the interiors of writers' minds, raising, not only the question of that about which authors write (the subject matter or content), but also the question of the manner in which they write (their compositional methods). Because this phase does constitute a deeper journey into the mind of the writer, so much less can be known about it than might be known about either the initial or the concluding phases of literary production (Pre-Creative and Post-Creative), which are seemingly more open to direct research. Nonetheless, useful deductions can be made.

To Emerson, literature is a form that by its nature communicates a universal or intuitive insight, to a specific and receiving audience. In other words, literature provides a channel of communication or a conduit from a supposed higher source (for Emerson, the Oversoul) to a supposed receiving source, that is, to the mind of the writer and, by this means, to the Society or the cultural audience. Thus, like all else to Emerson, literature makes possible an outer expression to an audience of the inner impulse he calls the Oversoul. This view is inherently dualistic, because, on the one hand, Emerson seems to be saying with Plato[13] that the literary subject invariably comes to us from the Oversoul and as such is predetermined or foreordained by inscrutable laws we cannot deny, such as those governing our instinct for justice or our supposed, innate capacity for love. On the other hand, Emerson's observations suggest that the form in which these unavoidable concepts become expressed depends upon the capabilities of the creative individual or individuals who serve as the facilitating, receiving, focusing, or concretizing agents, or those who are ready to receive the transmission. Thus, seemingly, what is fixed or predictable, in Emerson's mind, is the literary content or subject matter transmitted from the Oversoul. Literature, being one of a myriad of artistic vehicles of expression (for instance, painting or music), is one way by which the truths of this Oversoul can be communicated to us. On the other hand, what is variable (and not fixed like the impulses from

---

[13] Plato (428BC – 347BC). Classical Greek philosopher, the most famous student of Socrates, and widely influential in Western culture and art.

the Oversoul) are the forms of these fixed concepts as they emerge from the mind of given human agents, because the resultant communication depends radically upon the dance between the Oversoul and the mind of the individual receivers or creators – the individual, and individualized, writers, unavoidably coloring or refracting the light to which they have access. Thus, Emerson would be not only interested in whether literary concepts are authentic, that is, originating from the highest possible source, but he is also concerned with the way in which these concepts are processed by the individual agents who receive and therefore channel these impulses to us, their audience.

Emerson's theory must consequently begin with an appreciation of the role of the Oversoul in any and all creation of importance, but this theory must then address the activity of those groups or individuals blessed with the capacity of providing or facilitating the creation of specific vehicles of expression. In this latter aspect of his theory, Emerson typically asserts that, within a given society, concepts are routinely stepped down or transmitted from the Oversoul only by a privileged few, who are the gifted thinkers of a generation.[14] Among these thinkers (the philosophers, scientists, priests, etc.) are the writers themselves. As might be assumed, all of these thinkers draw impulses directly from the Oversoul in such a way that these impulses become modified by personal qualities, qualities nonetheless indispensable to the selection, contextualizing, and communication of the higher concepts. In short, then, Emerson might be called a proto-structuralist, concerned not only with a fixed or universal source of meaning

---

[14] Again, this premise seems Platonic.

but also with the processes by which this meaning becomes modified or adjusted by the various types of creative agents. The above are obviously challenging concepts.

1. <u>The Oversoul and the Authentic Literary Subject</u>. It is obvious that Emerson places much emphasis upon the notion that literature draws its subjects ultimately from what he calls the Oversoul, in which all truth dwells. This is another way of saying that literature is one of the means by which universal wisdom can be transferred or transmitted to Civilization. Indeed, this vital function gives literature its special authority. If this is indeed literature's main function, then the overarching subjects of literature (though varied or variable) are actually predetermined. This material from the Oversoul is subtly imposed upon us, and, as such, can never be denied or ignored. The subjects of literature are thereby pre-existent in the writer's "higher" nature "and in all nature" [Emerson and Emerson (ix: 189-190)]. For Emerson, the literary subject is indispensable or unavoidable because it is governed by ancient yet inscrutable laws, older and more expansive than Humanity itself. The supremacy of these laws is attested to by the fact that they "remain unbroken by our defects" and are "upspringing like the arch of the sky, or like sunlight, which all the wind in the universe cannot blow away; high, old laws, round, unremoveable; self-executing ...." [Emerson and Emerson (viii: 305)] These laws demonstrate that "wit, and wise men, and good judgment whether a thing be so or no" [Emerson and Emerson (viii: 560)] are, in fact, institutions even more ancient than the Christian Church -- and presumably of any one church or system of beliefs. Thus, the sole fact of existence which the writer ponders, the sole subject of literature, is this "invisible and imponderable" mystery [Emerson and Emerson (viii: 536)]. The writer explores "that which is its own evidence; which is self-executing; which cannot be conceived not to be; that which sets aside you and me, and can very well let us drop; and not we it." For instance, literature "could not deny the existence of justice, of love, of the laws of time and space" [Emerson and Emerson (ix: 189 - 90)], even if it were to cast doubt upon the existence and history of Christ. Paradoxically, despite the opportunity of a multitude of many thinkers to observe them over thousands of years, these laws remain inscrutable to the individual because, just as human life is too short to understand all there is to know even of human existence[Emerson and Emerson (x: 140 - 41)] so, "[n]o one has lived long enough to exhaust," let alone grasp, these mysteries [Emerson and Emerson (X: 444)].

Retaining their connections to Nature, all writers can do is use their instincts to shape the subject matter Nature provides. For, all "that gives currency still to any book published . . . by Little and Brown is the remains of faith in the breast of [all] that not adroit book-makers, but the inextinguishable soul of the Universe, reports of itself in articulate discourse through this and that other [individual], today, as of old...." [Emerson and Emerson (v: 282 - 84)] This fact, this "law of literature, give[s] its exact worth to every ballad and spoken sentence...." Thus, through literature, a "healthy light comes upon the mind ..." from Nature [Emerson and Emerson (ix: 400 - 01)].

2. The Variety of Creative Thinkers. But, we may ask, what is the connection between this Oversoul and human society in general? In any society, there will be found many accomplished thinkers, whose influence, in turn, elevates the level of thought in a given generation and causes unifying perceptions to circulate in a given culture, helping even to create among humans, collectively, a uniform character. Through these agents, the light of the Oversoul is circulated throughout Society as a whole, and also globally, and their collective insights may be said to create over-arching architectonic perceptions, to which people throughout the world may be widely receptive. Perceptions from the Oversoul are stepped down primarily by such individuals who, through maturity and skill, are able to rise to meet the Oversoul on its own level. Emerson implies that the materials offered by the Oversoul can be extracted only by individuals who can tap these ideas. These individuals assert that such "ideas are powers..." [Emerson and Emerson (viii: 402)] more important than matter. Their philosophy invariably dictates that things spiritual are "greater than any material force; that thoughts rule the world." Through these tenets they acquire the power to perceive and understand Being. Stated differently, such thinkers force themselves to come to terms with a keen question: Which are the realities, the thoughts or the iron spikes? And who is truly wanted, the railroad engineer or the philosopher?" They believe that people "of thought and of truth to thought are always wanted and for all ages [Emerson and Emerson (ix: 175)]; and that Archimedes and Kant are "as much realists as blacksmiths are."[15] In fact, Emerson says, these individuals "deal with intellections as rigorously and drastically as [joiners] with … chisel and board...." [Emerson and Emerson (viii: 210)] But, because of their belief in the primacy of ideas, these thinkers are often isolated from their generation, since they spend their lifetime answering

---

[15] Archimedes of Syracuse (288 BC – 212 BC). Greek Mathematician and Astronomer. -- Kant, Immanuel (1724 - 1804). Influential German philosopher and originator of the school of Transcendental idealism.

questions which we are not even qualified to pose -- questions of which their contemporaries seem to remain oblivious. And as a result, "the whole battle of the world is fought" in their heads, whose slightly "finer order" or slightly "larger angle of vision commands centuries of facts and millions of stupid people." Emerson boldly asserts, in fact, that the more of such "competent heads" there are in a civilization, the better all will fare [Emerson and Emerson (vii: 102)]. These individuals are especially successful transmitters of divine ideas because they evidence skill and spiritual maturity lacking in the majority, who, to Emerson, are still too young spiritually to understand how to draw upon the Oversoul. Hence, Emerson observes, "To say, 'the majority are wicked,' means no malice, nor bad heart in the observer, but simply that the majority are young, … are animals, and have not yet any opinion, but borrow their opinion of the newspaper, and, of course, are not worth considering: they have not yet come to themselves, do not yet know their opinion. That, if they knew it, is an oracle of God, and worthy of all curiosity and respect from them, and from all" [Emerson and Emerson (viii: 508)].

Because individuals of thought value Being, Emerson calls them heroes, before whom the "world is awed" and "subdued without knowing why" [Emerson and Emerson (ix: 343)]. They are useful to culture because they are actually able to rise to the level of the Oversoul. Emerson even observes that, since Nature (the vehicle of the Oversoul) "never alters," the grasping of the principles of science is not sequential or "chronological" but dependent upon the health of the inquirer [Emerson and Emerson (viii: 478)]. Hence, the "doctrine of Copernicus is not in one [person], but in the air, and whenever [thinkers have] larger lungs, [dilate] enough to breathe universal air, [they] also and suddenly [become] Copernican. Archimedes, Newton, Euclid, Laplace,

28

Bacon, are ample and think adequately to Nature .... And so often amid myriads of invalids, fops, dunces, and all kinds of damaged individuals, one sound healthy brain will be turned out, in symmetry, and relation to the system of the world: -- eyes that can see, ears that can hear, soul that can feel, mind that can receive the resultant truth" [Emerson and Emerson (viii: 478 - 79)].[16]

Accordingly, though Emerson declares that "every [one] carries ... the vision of the Perfect" [Emerson and Emerson (ix: 192)], not all of us are capable of recognizing or accessing this vision. Rather, the people who perceive this vision are often "the monotones," or individuals of one idea, exhibiting, "not poverty but a fruitful law," which is that only these seem "entitled to make the catalogue of powers and the order of genesis"; and without them, "the great primal powers will not sit for their portraits." [Emerson and Emerson (viii: 574 - 76)]. In short, though "[all have] the whole capital" in them and though each "knows all that Plato or Kant can teach" [Emerson and Emerson (ix: 185)], few possess the knowledge or discipline or have discovered the method of turning the key. Mainly the philosopher, the scholar, the writer and, without doubt, the theoretical scientist may turn this key; and even these are allowed to do so only tentatively [Emerson and Emerson (ix: 332)].

Evidently, too, there is a divine plan in the talents given to these individuals: "It is not for nothing that very few heads are sent into the world busy with abstractions, and very many heads

---

[16] Copernicus, Nicolaus (1473 - 1543). Famed Renaissance mathematician and astronomer, responsible in part for framing the Heliocentric theory. -- Newton, Sir Isaac (1643 - 1727). British mathematician and astronomer who early articulated what came to be known as the law of gravity. -- Euclid of Alexandria (4th Century BC?? – 270 BC?). Greek mathematician and founder of Euclidean geometry. -- Laplace. Pierre-Simon, Marquis de Laplace (1749 - 1847). French scientist, mathematician, and man of letters. -- Bacon, Sir Francis (1561 - 1626). Influential British philosopher, author, and early empiricist.

busy making money" [Emerson and Emerson (viii: 557)]. At any time, it only needs the contemporaneous appearance of a few [of these] superior and attractive [people] to give a new and noble turn to the public mind" [Emerson and Emerson (x: 9 - 10)], which ever bends towards the transcendent, thereby assuring "the certainty with which the best opinion comes to be the established opinion" [Emerson and Emerson (x: 68-69)] and guaranteeing that "there will always be a class of imaginative [individuals], whom poetry, whom the love of Beauty leads to the adoration of the moral sentiment...." [Emerson and Emerson (x: 9 - 10)] In light of the above, it is ever "the sure sign of national decay...when [such supposed] Brahmins can no longer read and understand the Brahminical science and philosophy" [Emerson and Emerson (viii: 558 - 59)].

These individuals not only serve as a conduit from the Oversoul to the cultures to which they belong, but their activity inevitably fosters links among cultures. For instance, the number of truly original thinkers is so small that there seemingly has developed a uniformity of perception among humanity, from the few ideas which these thinkers have been able to convey. This fact alone may explain why only a few ideas seem to prevail throughout the cultures of the earth, why these ideas tend to create a common intellectual architecture among humanity, and why therefore it appears that only one person wrote all the books. Even more, in any given era only a few thoughts seem to impress or rise to public consciousness (despite the innumerable books), just as, "though the stars appear so numberless, you cannot count more than a thousand" [Emerson and Emerson (ix: 134 - 35)]. Thus, to Emerson, the fact that the world entertains only a few striking generalizations [Emerson and Emerson (viii: 494)] not only denotes the presence of an underlying intellectual architecture but also explains why, transcending time, the theses of new writers can always be found in old books. We have to come to terms with the fact that "[e]very new writer is only a new crater of an old volcano" [Emerson and Emerson (ix: 555-56)], even though each new writer always seems stunned by the striking accuracy with which earlier authors have described what [was] wrongly thought ... a "new continent in the west." Such writers (no matter how ancient) become instantly modern when through their work they illustrate the all-encompassing effects of the laws of life and reason [Emerson and Emerson (ix: 469)]. Such ancient works express the universal truths, "what all sects accept" [Emerson and Emerson (x: 467)], in the same sense that Plato and the Bhagavad Gita are transnational and represent "chief structure[s] of human wit, like karnac ...." [Emerson and Emerson (vii: 86)][17] Indeed, again, it appears "that one [person] wrote all the books of literature" [Emerson and Emerson (iv: 478; vi: 465)]. Partaking of the same grand ideas of religion and morals, "Viasa and Swedenborg and Pythagoras see the same thing" [Emerson and Emerson (viii: 446-47)].[18] This one voice is also found, for instance, in Goethe,[19] whose "sincerity ... makes the value of literature" [Emerson and Emerson (vi: 466)]. To Emerson, the universality of thought, and ultimately the universality of character, is strikingly illustrated by the realization that "Michel Angelo and Raphael in the next age reappeared as Milton and Shakespeare" [Emerson and Emerson (viii:

---

[17] Bhagavad Gita. 2nd Century BCE Sanskrit text, part of the epic *Mahabharata*, and one of the most famous of the Hindu scriptures. -- Karnac. A massive temple complex near Luxor, Egypt, the construction of which extended over a vast period, from about 2000 BC – 30 BC.

[18] Vyasa. Legendary compiler of the *Mahabharata*. – Swedenborg, Emanuel (1688 - 1772). Swedish philosopher, theologian, and mystic, best known for his book *Heaven and Hell*, on the afterlife. -- Pythagoras of Samos (570BC? – 495BC?). Greek mathematician, philosopher, and astronomer.

[19] Goethe, Johann Wolfgang von (1749 - 1832). Premier German Romantic poet, statesman, and author of *Faust* and other works.

31

258)] and that "[e]very body would paint like Raffaelle, if everybody could paint at all" [Emerson and Emerson (x: 49)].[20]

In sum, this far-reaching perceptual unity promotes common institutions and a common character among Humanity. Because the "mask of Nature is variety," "our education is through surfaces and particulars; and multitudes remain in the babe or animal state, and never see or know more: but in the measure in which there is wit, we learn that we are alike; that a fundamental unity or agreement exists, without which there could be neither marriage, nor politics, nor literature, nor science" [Emerson and Emerson (ix: 168)]. Thus, despite the many differences which confront us, we are in practice, One Mind, and therefore, really one community, partaking of the same character [Emerson and Emerson (v: 446)]. And this unity exists because of the uniform human access to the Oversoul brought about by the "knowing" few, who are able to transmit their knowledge directly or indirectly to the many.

3. <u>The Writer as One of the "Knowing" Few</u>. If we leave the general consideration of thinkers and focus, instead, upon the one of interest here, we come upon an even sharper picture of the process by which the subject matter or content of a literary work is accessed or by which it is initiated in the mind of the writer. This notion, of "accessibility" to a subject or the issue of how a

---

[20] Michel Angelo or Michelangelo di Lodovico Buonarroti Simoni (1475 - 1564). Influential poet, painter, and sculptor of the Italian High Renaissance. -- Raffaelle/Raphael or Raffaello Sanzio da Urbino (1483 - 1520). Painter and architect of the Italian High Renaissance. -- Milton, John (1608 - 1674). Poet, Puritan religious theorist, and author of *Paradise Lost*. – Shakespeare, William (1564 – 1616). Often referred to as "The Bard of Avon," and author of many famous plays and poems, he is considered the most prolific writer in the English language.

subject comes to the writer, is a crucial one in the Emersonian universe, because Emerson never presumes to impinge upon the freedom of the writer by asserting that she or he should pursue this or that topic, subject matter, or concern. This choice is solely and irrevocably within the province of the individual writer. Rather, Emerson is interested only in how this registration comes about. As noted above, the most important point which Emerson seems to make is that literature is one of many conduits or vehicles by which wisdom is transmitted from the Oversoul – in this case, to writers and through them to readers and thereby to a given culture. This fact of transmission from the Oversoul endows the writer with certain powers, places at the forefront of his mind certain goals, and evokes from him a fundamental courage. These can also be regarded as skills which the writer must master.

a. The Writer's Power. Authors are endowed with a special power which ultimately makes civilizations possible and which thereby makes writers the people's ideal. Accessing this power depends upon the first skill that the writer must employ – that of discrimination. This is primarily a mental adjustment. Writers discover what are the best subjects; they discover that which links humanity to these subjects; and they actively build this link by relating the abstract and concrete, which is the ultimate methodology of all art, including writing. The process can be reduced to three activities, then: discovering the right subject, acknowledging ways in which this subject is relevant to the human condition, and rendering that subject in concrete terms so that it can make an impact.

Discovery. The writer discovers rather than creates subjects. Emerson asserts, with respect to literary subject matter, that art "lies not in making your object prominent, but in choosing objects that are prominent" [Emerson and Emerson (viii: 253)]. This suggests that the subject is not invented but discovered. Emerson observes, writers that adhere "to modes of wants that can be dispensed with, [go] out of fashion, [build their] house off the road. But [the one] who addresses ... problems that [all] must come to solve, builds [a] house on the road, and [all] must come to it. Jesus's problems are mine, and therefore to Jesus and through Jesus must we go, and Swedenborg had the like wisdom" [Emerson and Emerson (viii: 63)]. Putting themselves in the position to discern these subjects requires constant effort from writers: "Just as [all are] conscious of the law of vegetable and animal nature," Emerson observes," so the sensitive inquirer is "aware of an Intellect which overhangs his consciousness like a sky; of degree above degree; and heaven within heaven. Number is lost in it. Millions of observers could not suffice to write its first law. Yet it seems to him...as if gladly he would dedicate himself to such a god...." [Emerson and Emerson (viii: 567 - 68)] Hence, of his own labor, Emerson observes: "I write laboriously after a law, which I see, and then lose, and then see again. And, I doubt not ... that my reader will do me justice to feel that I am not contriving something to surprise or to tickle him, but am seriously striving to say that which is" [Emerson and Emerson (ix: 468)]. It is obvious from our discussion of the variety of creative thinkers, above, that for Emerson all that civilization is or can become arises from the individual creator, "the inventor, the worth giver," who in turn is a reflection of the Divine Creator, Who brings about at all times "the Divine Newness" [Emerson and Emerson (x: 189 - 90)], a "newness" which must always be an essential feature of anything the writer creates. This is why "the ideal of any people is in their best writers, sculptors, painters, and builders, in their greatest heroes and creators in any and every kind" [Emerson and Emerson (viii: 359)].

Value to Humanity. Emerson sees that writers not only "discover" their subject, but that they, after discovering this subject, must grasp its meaning or value to Humanity. They know why for us the subject is magnetic, vital. They know not only that we need to understand a certain truth but also why we need to understand it. After writers "[draw] out of the invisible [their] material," they then play their "game by a skill not taught or quickened by [their] appetites" [Emerson and Emerson (v: 262 - 63)]. At first, the subject is nothing more than an "hypothesis, or algebraic, or unknown quantity," but its relevance to Humanity is "the truth" that must "be arrived at" [Emerson, Journals (viii: 419)]. This truth, once known, becomes a "firm line" which will remain "like the names of discoverers of planets, written in the sky in letters which could never be obliterated" [Emerson and Emerson (vii: 208)]. Those who use logic or "semblances of logic," to find out this truth, invariably fail, while the poet, by virtue of a connection with the Oversoul, "knows the missing link at once, as the lapidary knows the true stone from glass and paste" [Emerson and Emerson (viii: 419)].

Concretization. Beyond discovering a subject and understanding its significance or value, the writer must grasp the principle by which all art is externalized. This is a more practical side of dealing with a subject and one that is needed to bring about results. The writer comes to appreciate the role which a strange dualism (an only-apparent antagonism) plays in the health and growth of creative work. Emerson observes this ability to bridge from the higher to the lower in "the robust Greek mythology," which revealed a "cosmic" (or perhaps one should say, "astronomic") imagination. This mythology evidenced "a power ... of expressing in graceful fable the laws of the world, so that the mythology is beautiful poetry on one side, at any moment convertible into severe science on the other...." [Emerson and Emerson (viii: 359 - 61)] And, according to Emerson, this mythology (and presumably mythology like it throughout the world) survives "to this day [because]...it is more catholic than" others [Emerson and Emerson (ix: 135)] and demonstrates the ability of writers as bridging or transmitting agents for the Oversoul. They come to understand that literature, as Emerson constantly has noted, cannot be divorced from its concrete origins in Nature but that, rather, there is a tantalizing correspondence and affiliation between Nature and art; and that on this perception of correspondence all the writer's work must be founded. In fact, Emerson perceives it to be one of the jobs of the writer to show more clearly the ways in which the "laws below are sisters of the laws above" [Emerson and Emerson (x: 204 - 06)]. The general method is thus immediately revealed when the writer discerns this natural marriage between Spirit and Matter, a marriage that helps authors to give their arts and thought a basis in the real world: "We must have a basis for our delicate entertainments of poetry and philosophy in our handicraft," Emerson asserts. "We must have an antagonism in the tough world for all the variety of our spiritual faculties or they will not be born" [Emerson and Emerson (v: 394)]. The writer consequently comes to regard "[e]very breath of air [as] the carrier of the Universal mind," and every part of Nature as an analog or symbol for every other part.

This dual procedure in literature seems inevitable because humanity, as well, has "two sets of faculties, the particular and the catholic, like a boat furnished with wheels for land and water travel. It is ever strange, an unfit marriage," since we are the children "of this most impossible marriage, this of the two worlds" [Emerson and Emerson (vi: 517)]. Elsewhere, Emerson draws a similar distinction, using it to differentiate talent from genius: "Some ... have the perception of difference predominant, and are conversant with surfaces and trifles, with coats and coaches, and faces, and cities; these are the [individuals] of talent .... And other[s] ... abide by the perception of Identity; these are the Orientals, the philosophers, the [individuals] of faith and divinity, [those] of genius" [Emerson and Emerson (vi: 493 - 94)]. Accordingly, "Talent says things ... never heard but once; and Genius, things ... never heard. Hence, genius is power; Talent is applicability. A human body, an animal, is an applicability; the Life, the Soul is Genius" [Emerson and Emerson (vi: 370 - 71)]. To Emerson, then, the "difference between writers is that one counts forms, and the other counts powers" [Emerson and Emerson (x: 109)], resulting also in two types of books -- one strong and healthy; the other, mediocre and ill: "Strong minds ask principles, direct apercus, and original forms. The sick public want what is secondary, conventional, and imitations of imitations" [Emerson and Emerson (x: 263)]. Thus, the writer is in the position to tap [the] higher self, to choose the right subjects as a result of communicating with this self, and through these subjects, to have (like the scientist, philosopher, or inspired engineer) a direct and original impact upon a culture. In the end, writers learn the method of transcendence, and it is this method which allows them to exert a positive influence upon Society. We see that poets are so rare because they "must be exquisitely fine and vital in [their] tissues, and at the same time immovably centered" [Emerson and Emerson (vii: 26)], aware of the dynamic substance above, yet open to sense experience below. This fact perhaps accounts for a peculiar phenomenon: For Emerson, it is understandable that poets like Wordsworth and William Ellery Channing[21] seem commonplace when you meet them; and we find it difficult to reconcile what we see of them with the poetry which they produce. It is as if there opens up "a chamber in [the] brain into which an angel flies with divine messages.... 'Ah, not to me these heights belong;/A better voice sings through my song'" [Emerson and Emerson (x: 360)]. Yet, the poetic gift is "as the breath and supremacy of man" and is particularly supreme when "the poet ... suffers the man to sit in him with the poet" [Emerson and Emerson (vii: 98)].

Admittedly, the issue of the transmission of the subject from the Oversoul to the writer, is obstruse. But an example may help to illustrate the assumed process. If, first of all, the subject that is impressed upon the writer concerns the concept of Compassion, the writer, second of all, must understand the value of this concept to Humanity – that is to say, why Humanity needs to express this quality at a given time. The writer, after this need is intuitively understood, must, third of all, find out how to express this concept in images, symbols, dramatic demonstrations, and by any other means by which it can be grasped by the audience mentally and emotionally, using the tools to be found in Nature, the expansive vehicle of the intuition. Later, when we turn to literary construction (Chapter 4, "Literary

---

[21] Wordsworth, William (1770 - 1850). One of the founders of the British Romantic movement and an influential poetic theorist. -- Channing, William Ellery (1818 - 1901). Considered one of the more promising Transcendental poets.

Form"), it will be possible to amplify this topic of correspondence.

b. The Writer's Goal. Transmission from the Oversoul is naturally affected by the writer's main goal. Constantly struggling to retain his connections to the Oversoul, all the writer can do is use intuition and instinct to shape the subject matter which this higher influence provides. This process of "shaping" what the Oversoul provides results in a work which communicates something of value. The problem has to do with the specifics of how this transmission takes place, and we are therefore left with wondering what the specific challenge is, what the writer must consider in confronting this challenge, and what are the solutions. All of these issues have to do with the capacity of the writer to receive this transmission. In other words, all have to do with the writer's unique lens and the capacity of the writer to adjust this lens to receive the communication.

Instinctively and inexactly, the author is one who struggles with this inscrutable dance between the Oversoul and the individual consciousness, which constantly attempts to perceive this sublime message, so that the writer can later transmit this message to his audience. The mere witnessing of the operations of Nature which takes place in the mind of the writer initiates a chain reaction which leads instantly to poetry: It "is noble[;] it is poetic, and makes poets, only to have seen [these operations] -- to have computed their curve." This chain reaction which takes place in the mind of writers renders superfluous their reliance (like the average citizen) unduly upon the insights of fellow thinkers in their generation; rather, the writer must enjoy "his [own] root in Nature [and draw] his [own] power directly from it.... He must be such that, set him down where you will, he shall find himself at home, shall see how he can wave his useful lines here as there, and make himself necessary to society by the method in his [own] brain...." [Emerson and Emerson (ix: 400 - 01)]

The Writer's Lens. Writers clear their lenses, that is, reconcile the light of the Oversoul and their capacity to receive this light, by adhering to an unavoidable discipline. Although writers receive their primary inspiration from the Oversoul, it cannot be denied that this inspiration is colored or modified by the writer's mind and personality, which are largely reflective of influence from a culture and from the minds of the people in it. It goes without saying that all writers are deeply influenced by these contexts (by the culture in which their talent unfolds and by their own personality). We have to take into account, therefore, that the inspiration received from the Oversoul is invariably modified by the writer's cultural consciousness, which constitutes by necessity an individual lens, and the question that then arises is, what goes to create this lens, this unique prism.

First, one powerful aspect is the very culture of writers, which means the people in it, their family, their social group, and their national perspective or global identity. This involves many assumptions, values, modes of feeling, and habits of response of which the writer is in effect often unconscious. An example would be writers' clueless depiction of women as passive or of a Latin as passionate simply because these writers have not yet grown beyond the prejudices of their culture. These defects will appear in their work, as an aspect of their individual lens, and thereby, the transmission from the Oversoul gets somewhat distorted.

A second aspect of this lens (and another source of distortion) is what is contributed by writers' own personality, their tendencies and predispositions. Examples would be authors' limited or expansive command of language affecting their ability to express accurately what they feel or have seen or their limited or expansive imagination reflecting their level of education or their degree of sensitivity. These factors will always condition the sophistication of what is written and act as a modifying prism.

A third influence is the literary canon dominant during the period of their formation as writers. The influence of this canon we will discuss at length, later. What we can acknowledge now is that here is where writers often derive their initial artistry or aesthetic sensibility. What is the source of their style? By what models, if any, have they shaped their work? What are their other aesthetic tendencies? Will contemporary critiques play a part in clouding or sharpening their lens?

The Writer's Impartiality. Writers reconcile the light of the Oversoul and their capacity to receive it (their lens) by adhering to the discipline of impartiality. As they come to grasp this challenge of reception, their consciousness struggles to untie their personal Gordian knots, which is how to make effective this link between the Oversoul and their consciousness. When it comes to untying this knot, to unpacking how to create this desired link, what is paramount is the writer's ability to temper personal idiosyncrasies or biases by the necessary discipline which distinguishes an honest creator from one of bad faith, as Sartre puts it.[22] Only through detachment can the writer prepare the ground for authentic insights, which means those of integrity. The writer is left to her or his own devices, to achieve this goal.

---

[22] Jean-Paul Charles Aymard Sartre (1905 - 1980). One of the founders of Existentialism.

That is to say, writers are left with the arduous task of finding, in their personal make up and with the aid (or hindrance) of their individual lens, a way or ways of "connecting," of speaking with a voice that is universal and not private. Ultimately, then, writers, through their own relationship with the Oversoul, must become direct transmitters of ideas, ostensibly by drawing upon qualities which can blend this personal lens with the influences of the Oversoul. This is a deep-seated conflict. As suggested above, the problem is wholly on the side of the writers, because they are tasked always with finding the Oversoul and making themselves its channel. Writers must condition themselves to receiving the Oversoul but not the other way around. Thus, the second skill which the writer must develop to become a better conduit of the Oversoul, is impartiality or detachment. And this adjustment is, for all intents and purposes, emotional in nature. In point of fact, the writer is taking a critical step beyond that of the previous effort of merely understanding the marriage between higher and lower, between concrete and abstract, between material and spiritual, by gaining or enforcing the perspective needed for effective work. In this effort, they must do three things: a. choose the higher pole of the pair of opposites, which is central to the methodology of literature; b. grasp thereby a vision of the whole; and c. endeavor to convey this vision undistorted to the public.

The writer's journey induces her or him to prefer one of the opposite poles of the pairs of opposites over the other.[23] This is

---

[23] Though one of Emerson's acknowledged proteges, Walt Whitman suggested that no such choice is necessary or even desirable – that, indeed, the so-called "higher" and "lower" are co-equal sides of one mystical whole. Emerson, on the other hand, takes the position that the so-called "higher," subjective, or interior is superior to, and needs to be chosen over, the so-called "lower," material, or objective. It is interesting how a similar dichotomy represented a main difference in our own time between Claude Levi-Strauss and his supposed protege Jacques Derrida. — Whitman, Walt (1819 – 1892). One of the most influential of the American poets, known especially for the ground-breaking free verse poem *Leaves of Grass*. – Levi-Strauss,

because the insights of the Oversoul always have an interior rather than exterior reference and use. As Emerson points out in his book *Nature*, the exterior (or Nature) is always a vehicle of or a language for the Oversoul. At any rate, because this dualism is inherent in the very consciousness of the writer, it has to be resolved -- but resolved in favor of the spiritual or moral rather than the material or expedient. This decision creates a division among writers, among whom there are two classes of minds: one, "delighting in a bounded fact," which characterizes appearance; the other, "in its relations or correspondency to all other facts" [Emerson and Emerson (viii: 501)], a correspondence which gives the writer a deeper, more intuitive insight into reality. This latter faculty implies "a kind of latent omniscience not only in every [one], but in every particle...." [Emerson and Emerson (ix: 300)]

It is a question of using this choice in favor of the higher, to bring writers to the higher ground on which they can directly contact the Oversoul. In order to make this choice, writers are forced to subordinate the personality, so that they can approach their task from as high a ground as possible, and learn to work from a vision of the whole. Although it is important to note that detachment allows the writer to subordinate personality, or the Emersonian lower principle, it is equally important to grasp that it should be piety, not pride, which leads to the suppression of the personality part of this pair [Emerson and Gilman (xiii: 452)]. In fact, the writer's failure to report Nature as Nature, rather than as colored excessively through individual eyes or the personal lens, "diminishes the attraction of the thing in a fatal manner" [Emerson and Emerson (x: 43)]. For the writer comes to realize that, in literature

---

Claude (1908 - 2009). One of the founders of structural anthropology. – Derrida, Jacques (1930 - 2004). French philosopher whose famous "re-reading" of Levi-Strauss, led to the post-structuralist and post-modern theory called deconstruction.

as in life" [e]verything connected with our personality fails ...."[24] [Emerson and Emerson (vii: 426)] The writer attains the higher ground needed to create in a way which will convince, and win the attention of, others -- as" [e]very man who would do anything well must come to it from a higher ground...." In the actual literary work, too, the writer achieves "a height which attracts more than other parts, and which is best remembered" [Emerson and Emerson (x: 276)]. In this, the author follows Nature, which "never draws the moral, but leaves it for the spectator" [Emerson and Emerson (vii: 190)]. Emerson observes that the "Celestial Mind" in the writer automatically treats "all with a sovereign equality"; and, for this reason, Homer[25] "never discovers in the Iliad a preference to the Greeks over the Trojans" [Emerson and Emerson (x: 277)]. Similarly, Shakespeare's [Emerson and Emerson (x: 23)][26] "impartiality ... is like that of the light itself, which is not aristocrat but shines as mellowly on gipsies, as on emperors, on bride and corpse, on city and swamp" [Emerson and Emerson (viii: 62)]. When he observes that "No one who writes or utilizes his opinions can possibly be fair," Emerson is, therefore, addressing the question of distance, detachment, perspective, and universality -- which he finds to be innate to the soundest writing [Emerson and Emerson (x: 101)].[27] Allowing one to escape from this personal prism, detachment (and detachment alone) is the door

---

[24] Perhaps this is the distinction made by Friedrich Schiller, when he speaks of the difference between the "naive" and "sentimental" writer. Some readers will find also interesting the comparison with John Keats' "negative capability."

[25] Homer. The supposed author of both the *Iliad* and the *Odyssey*.

[26] The reader will note that Emerson is totally enamored of Shakespeare, finding in him the quintessential artist. This admiration is evidenced in Emerson's constant reference to Shakespeare and his relentless use of Shakespeare's work as an absolute standard against which to judge all other writers. Indeed, to Emerson, literary criticism is nothing more than a making of rules out of Shakespeare's "beauties."

[27] As well, we shall see, to the soundest literary criticism.

through which a thing becomes original, a quality that is nothing more than the habit of the thinker or maker to recur "to universal views" [Emerson and Emerson (ix: 173)].

The Writer's Undistorted Vision. Thus, the true nature of such writers is revealed, not only in their subject matter, but also in their detached point of view in presenting that subject matter: "Would you know the genius of the Writer, do not enumerate his talents or his feats, but ask thyself what spirit he is of? Has he led thee to Nature because his own soul was too happy in beholding her power and love? or has he only shown you stars and mountains, woods and lovely forms as his house, bribing you by the splendor of his palace to come and see him? .... The water we wash with will never speak of itself, nor does fire, or wind, or tree. Neither does the noble natural man; he yields himself to your occasion and use, but his act expresses a reference to universal good" [Emerson and Emerson (v: 347 - 48)]. Since "the soul of the world" is in all of us, "we require [this] absoluteness in every soul, --absoluteness in the orator, -- in the poet, -- in the hero, -- in all manners; and if they have it not, they simulate it" [Emerson and Emerson (x: 186)]. Consequently, writers must learn what Emerson calls "detachment by illumination," which allows artists to execute their work [Emerson and Emerson (ix: 309)] while removing themselves from the picture. Otherwise, the personality point of view creates a bias of perception, and that bias becomes all, as in the case of a farmer or soldier or real-estate broker, who, seeing the same plot of land, will understand and dispose of that plot fanatically and in entirely different ways [Emerson and Emerson (x: 146-47)]. Such variations in perspective are so significant because the "'eye altering alters all.'" Emerson admits that, though we applaud and find power in writers who offer "to stand deputy for the human race" and to write all of their "secret history colossally out as philosophy," yet when these writers fail to bring off this feat and appear "morbid" or "partially sick," their efforts seem "odious" [Emerson and Emerson (v: 446)]. For this same reason, it disturbs us "when poets, who are by excellence the thinking and feeling of the world, are deficient in truth of intellect and of affection. Then is Feeling unfeeling and Thought unwise" [Emerson and Emerson (vi: 369)]. In fact, the poem is a good one precisely because the writer's ends are "remote." The poem "is not written to any person or moment, but to life generalized and perspectived." The writer does not live by the same calendar as the banker, but by the sidereal time of cause and consequence" [Emerson and Emerson (viii: 513)].

This higher ground puts in the hand of the writer the ability to seek a vision of the whole, a vision that is certainly grander, more exalted, than art itself. For, a "great cosmical intellect is indifferent to the arts, may easily look at them as poor toys, as … at a child's picture-alphabet." Even so, vision of the whole and the detection of design in Nature are the goals of the saint's "grand healthy perception" [Emerson and Emerson (x: 186)]. And being so exalted, this goal of the saint readily becomes the writer's own because "In some sort the end of life is that [one] should take up the universal into [oneself]" [Emerson and Emerson (viii: 257)]. This notion that writing seeks to augment or support the role of the saint, in fact, becomes one of the prominent concepts in Emerson's whole notion of the value and impact of literature. This "generalized" and haunting perspective induced by the detachment which writers bring to their work, is inevitably where literature, at its very heart, seeks to lead us: "Cannot all literature, and all our own remote experience avail to teach us that the to-day which seems so trivial, the task which seems so unheroic,

46

the inexpressive blank look of the present moment...cannot all avail to teach us that these are wholly deceptive appearances, and that as soon as their recoverable years have placed their Blue between these and us, these things shall glitter and attract us, seeming to be the wildest romance, and -- as far as we allowed them in passing to take their own way and natural shape -- the homes of beauty and poetry?" [Emerson and Emerson (v: 514)]

c. <u>The Writer's Courage</u>. Ultimately, in addition to arriving at an understanding of their power and in maintaining the related detachment that is required, writers need courage. And this adjustment seems primarily physical, expressing what we often call "intestinal fortitude." Courage allows writers to acknowledge that there will be opposition, to acquire the power to face off this opposition, and to accept a probable isolation -- simply because what they are attempting to express frequently conflicts with the current ideas of society.

Society's Opposition. Society often interprets original communications or the asserting of new principles as declarations of war against what is known and established. Thus, in the eyes of the conventional thinker, every "principle is a war note. Whoever attempts to carry out the rule of right and love and freedom must take his life in his hand" [Emerson and Emerson (ix: 249; ix: 362)]. There is, therefore, something heroic in the lives of those who attempt to link the spiritual and the mundane. This is because "[b]etween poetry and prose must the great gulf yawn ever and they who try to bridge it over" are regarded by their contemporaries as "lunatics or hypocrites" [Emerson and Emerson (vii: 335)]. Emerson concludes that "[o]ur people mean that [individuals] of thought shall be dilettanti; ornamental merely; if

47

they dare to be practical with their ideas of beauty, it is on their peril" [Emerson and Emerson (viii: 212 -13)]. "Thus, is it not unusual that the wisest and noblest in any culture would find themselves denounced by their own sects, and sustained by these believed adversaries of their sects?"

Heroic Response. For all of these reasons, Emerson respects courage. He likes people "of will and of thought because there is nobody behind [their] chair" [Emerson and Emerson (ix: 223)]. This "[c]ourage charms us, because it indicates that [people love] an idea better than all things in the world, that [they are] thinking neither of [their] bed, nor … dinner, nor … money, but will venture all to put in act the inevitable thought of [their minds]" [Emerson and Emerson (ix: 246)]. This quality makes the individual willing to challenge those static precepts of society at whatever cost to themselves: "Here and there is a soul which is a seed or principle of good, a needle pointing to the true north, thrown into the mountains of foolishness …. and deserts of evil …. This soul has the secret of power, this soul achieves somewhat new and beautiful which endears heaven and earth to mankind and lends a domestic grace to the sun and the stars" [Emerson and Emerson (viii 255 - 56)]. Thankfully, then, "the too dark ground of history is starred over with solitary heroes who dared to believe better of their brothers and who prevailed by actually executing in some part the law (the high ideal) in their own life, and though a hissing and an offence to their contemporaries, yet they became a celestial figure to all succeeding souls as they journeyed through nature. How shine the names of Abraham, Diogenes,

Pythagoras, and the transcendent Jesus in antiquity" [Emerson and Emerson (vii: 335)].[28]

The Writer's Consequent Courage. One cannot help noting the similarity between this strength of character and the courage needed by the writer, who, among other conflicts, struggles with the pair of opposites on which writing stands. Emerson finds that it is this very struggle to express divinity or the Oversoul which characterizes the best authors. These are able to transmit the aims of the soul, which, in seeking a "far future consummation..., reacts through ages, and ennobles and beautifies every modern moment, and makes the individual great among ... coevals, though they had every advantage of skill, force, and favor" [Emerson and Emerson (viii:255 - 56)]. A writer must exhibit the "courage which is grand, the courage to feel that Nature who made me may be trusted, and one's self painted as also a piece of Nature...." [Emerson and Emerson (viii: 250 - 51)] Although the writer may be "ostracized" [Emerson and Emerson (x: 234)] or "maligned and isolated by the rest" [Emerson and Emerson (viii: 255)], only such courage can make effective the writer's efforts to share insights with the rest of society. All of their exulted effort may be short-circuited or even destroyed, if writers lack the essential courage to follow through with what has been granted them.

In summary, then, the practical goal of the writer is the same as that of thinkers such as the scientists, philosophers, and other conduits who dare to open through their own efforts the flood gates of the Oversoul. This is the grand service which they provide to society. Writers open this channel for the audience.

---

[28] Abraham. Biblical Patriarch. -- Diogenes (412 BC? – 323 BC). Greek philosopher and a founder of the school of Cynics.

But it is worth noting that they can do so only through the lens of impartiality. They cannot properly do this through personal blinders which cover up or distort the message. When we stand back and consider the whole, we realize that writers' supposed courage is resonant throughout the whole because it has been a courage that is three-fold in nature: the mental courage to grasp the nature and value of their contribution, emotional courage to get out of their own light and to allow the Oversoul to pass through them unchanged, and the intestinal fortitude (as we call it) to face all opposition that prevents them from stepping down this message to the audience that awaits it.

Though it is critical for us to understand how literary subject matter comes to the writer from the Oversoul, an equally significant element of the literary process is the writer's ability to embody these subjects into some type of tangible form, thereby giving others access to insights which would otherwise remain trapped within the writer's consciousness. Emerson has earlier pointed out that the writer's initial formulation of these insights requires the ability to recognize the pairs of opposites, the ability to be impartial, and the ability to demonstrate personal courage in presenting these concepts to the public. This seems basically what we mean when we speak loosely of Inspiration. But writers, if they are to externalize these concepts beyond the initial transmission from the Oversoul, need a complementary and more plastic rather than primarily intuitive ability – the capacity to use the mind, not only as a conduit for the Oversoul, but also as a resource for the construction of the literary vehicle itself. The primary tools of this more plastic and admittedly less intuitive work are writers' executive ability, which enables them to use the intellect to guide the construction from inception to completion; an abundant creative imagination, by which they can envision the project in all of its points of growth; and unending compositional skill, which allows them to bring into expression that which has been imagined. All of these go hand in hand. Stated more directly, executive ability is necessary to help hold the project steady. Imagination embodies the very power of formation, in that it truly is the only tool which conceives the product into existence, if only as a creative potential.

51

Compositional skill goes beyond the conception held in the imagination of the writer by providing the form that the original intuition will inhabit, making it accessible to an audience.

1. <u>The Writer's Executive Ability</u>. The first complementary ability (dynamic by inference) which the writer needs is executive ability – the ability mentally to do three things: to focus attention on the task of construction, to accept the likelihood of failure if Nature Itself is the standard, and to exercise a day-to-day discipline until the task is accomplished. All of these skills enable the writer to overcome an inherent inertia that plagues everything on our earth both physical and mental. This is akin to the rocket's ability to overcome the gravitational pull of earth. But here we must remember that these skills and others cannot possibly express themselves sequentially and that the notion of sequence creeps into every narrative as a convenience of explanation. Rather, these skills unfold simultaneously and continuously throughout the whole effort of creation, in the same way, I would assert, that in the human body the brain function, the heart function, and the digestive function are simultaneous, not sequential. This is a caveat that must be remembered at every point of the discussion.

a. <u>Power of Focus</u>. The writer has to ex-press, or literally, to push out by a focused attention or to press out, the vision or intuition from the Oversoul so that this vision can ultimately end in some type of completed form. Emerson's basic contention is that, without this type of conscious focus, without the ability to *embody* insights from the Oversoul, the writer's goal cannot be realized. The issue can be understood if the writer: 1.

acknowledges the problem of transition, from perception to vehicle, 2. understands how critical or valued this skill of transition is, and 3. accepts that this skill derives from participation in one of the many powers of God.

From Perception to Vehicle. Sadly, Nature does not confer equally the power to express, even if the writer possesses the ability to perceive light from the Oversoul. Indeed, adequate power both to perceive and to express what is perceived is "not oftcn cntrusted to the same hand," as the "hands to complete are not often given to the seeing soul," which, though "filled with vision," lacks discipline and is "careless of its slow fulfillment in events" [Emerson and Emerson (ix: 409-10)]. Thus, vision alone, falls short in the creative process; for art not only requires perception by what Emerson calls a living soul [Emerson and Emerson (vii: 33)]; it also requires an adequate vehicle by which to convey that perception. This dual need of vision and vehicle may account for the paucity of successful writers, because a writer not only must struggle to discover the truth but also strive to embody it [Emerson and Emerson (vii: 113)]. In this way, the genius of many has been nullified simply from their inability to give form to vision

Value of Transition. This nullification of genius because of the inability to provide an adequate form for vision, constitutes a failure to value the importance of transition or bridging while pursuing the creative cycle. It is nothing more than a failure of a law of Nature which requires expulsion of all that is ingested. In fact, it may be that some writers do not necessarily have deeper insight than do others: it may be that the former do not allow thoughts to "be pent and smouldered and noxious" but permit them to "pass over into new forms," thereby following the hygeian precept to "Keep the body open" [Emerson and Emerson (x: 171)]. It is a matter of breaking "through the fence of silence" and finding in an appropriate vehicle the needed voice that can give vent to the originating insight [Emerson and Emerson (v: 237-238)]. Writers who are unable to bridge between perception and vehicle, remain "linear" and feel "incomplete"; but no sooner than they find an outlet in "times" and "events," they "round" [Emerson and Emerson (viii: 230)]. Hence, to Emerson, expression can be said to be nothing more than "a healthy perspiration and growth" [Emerson and Emerson (vii: 279)]. By way of illustration, Emerson says, Shakespeare's genius for expression makes him sweat "like a haymaker, all pores" [Emerson and Emerson (vii: 279-80)].

This difficulty of bridging between insight and expression makes one think that "Nature distributed vulgar beauty unequally, as if she did not value it; but the most precious beauty she put in our own hands, that of expression" [Emerson and Emerson (x: 229)]. Expression must be precious because all celebrate this power in others. When the people hear the poet or sayer of the old psalms or gospel, who speaks "with a kind of perfection," they declare, "Thus saith the Lord" [Emerson and Emerson (x: 171)]; and they "forgive every crime" to those who exhibit similar powers [Emerson and Emerson (vi: 84-85)]. Indeed, they beg such persons to represent and rule them [Emerson and Emerson (viii: 148)]. For Emerson, proof that Humanity values the creative person "precisely in proportion to his power of expression" is, again, the fact that to Shakespeare "they have awarded the highest place" [Emerson and Emerson (viii: 71)].

Participation in a Divine Power. Just as physical gravity holds bodies and any object to the earth, requiring some type of counter-physical propulsion to free them to soar above the fated influence of the earth's gravitational pull, so writers must discover within themselves a parallel, counter and mental propulsion that allows them to break free from the fixed mental influences hindering them from being creators in their own right. They realize that, to do this, they must draw from, be part of, or mimic the capacities that empower God to create. The possible key to achieving this mental propulsion is suggested by Emerson in "Intellect" (*Essays :First Series*): "[T]he intellect dissolves fire, gravity, laws, method, and the subtlest unnamed relations of nature, in its resistless menstruum" [Emerson et al. (292)]. For this reason, the intellect is the tool that can allow writers to offset the inertia which prevents them from writing. Naturally, to Emerson, this intellect (like everything else) must be drawn from God. Yet, as neoclassical thinkers readily point out, human intellect is partial, imperfect, and merely a shadow or reflection of that demonstrated by God. Perhaps this is the point Emerson was attempting to make in Chapter V of *Nature* ("Discipline"), when he asserts that "[e]very particular in nature, a leaf, a drop, a crystal, a moment of time is related to the whole, and partakes of the perfection of the whole. Each particle is a microcosm, and faithfully renders the likeness of the world" [Emerson et al. (24)]. Implicit in these statements is a dual realization: 1. that man's intellect is, of course, partial; and 2. that, more importantly, this intellect partakes of or is an aspect of God's potency.

b. <u>Acquiescence to Failure</u>. Whatever sense of purpose writers bring to the task, they have to come to terms with the fact that any form produced by their divinely-given, but partial, intellect can only approximate (never adequately replicate or exceed) the presumably perfect forms created by God and observable in Nature. This recognition is certainly incident to the paradox, on the one hand, of the utter insignificance of human beings and, on the other, of their role as creative participants used by the Oversoul, making them co-creators. This notion certainly refers to the Emersonian doctrine of participation roughly related to the Hindu doctrine of darma or duty. All individuals have a responsibility towards and a unique placement in the Plan of God, and for Emerson, the more they discover and then embrace that unique position and work, the more they assist infinitesimally in what God creates. Thus, though in human terms all creative projects are always defective, limited, and imperfect, this perception of failure arises from the human inability to see or visibly to affect the big picture. Here, we see suggested the paradox confronting the biblical Job. His complaints arose from his inability to grasp what God readily knew and what God had the power readily to do. His complaints stem from the partiality of his perception and the relatively inconsequential nature of his power. Stated again, writers must accept that, despite this vaunted capacity of expression, their efforts of giving form to insights from the Oversoul will never reach perfection. This consequence is inevitable because, the basic difference between art (the product of humankind) and Nature (the product of God) is that, in comparison with Nature, art can gain only relative perfection or development and be "only relatively good; the artist advances, and finds all his fine things naught" [Emerson and Emerson (vi: 325)]. This consciousness of unavoidable failure is the reason alone that poets are ever "wretched" at their "shortcomings" [Emerson and Emerson (ix: 437)].

As despairing as all of this may sound, a bridgeless gulf between language and reality helps to create this humbling (or should we say, humiliating) difficulty: Initially, writers believe that finding the right name for an object is more important than

56

accessing the object to which the name refers. They seek the word which suggests the "humane and universal beauty, and significance of the object." If they have such a word, then they believe they have all that is important. It is true, as we shall see below, that Emerson's entire theory of creative development rests upon the notion of finding the right name for an object and of using that name as a way of controlling, if not triumphing over, an otherwise obtuse, intractable, and unassailable Nature. But the truth is that the process of construction involves using the intellect to create *an enchanted sphere*, in which literature is allowed to flourish. But this sphere, we come to realize, is a pitiful human fabrication. This observation perhaps suggests to us something of Emerson's understanding of literature, which is, as we have stated, the ability to reveal the inner meaning or significance of things; their true relationship to spiritual reality [Emerson and Emerson (x: 175-76)]. But in this theory of literature, we also have to include Emerson's skepticism as to the degree to which the human being is actually capable of perceiving – and for that matter, replicating -- this reality. Emerson knows that sentences are unavoidably exaggerated and hence false, in that they can only extract or "detach" limited meaning from "the infinite diffuseness," which "refuses to be epigrammatized...." Thus, though literature attempts to convey the inner significance of things, the bitter truth is that literature never can. It is always incomplete, inept, and partial [Emerson and Emerson (vi: 65)].[29]

We "learn with joy and wonder this new and flattering art of language, deceived by the exhilaration which accompanies the attainment of each new word. We fancy we gain somewhat. We gain nothing. It seemed ... that words come nearer to the thing;

---

[29] Perhaps this fact reinforces a main point of Derrida's theory of deconstruction.

described the fact; were the fact. [We] learn later that they only suggest it. It is an operose, circuitous way of putting us in mind of the thing -- of flagellating our attention. But this was slowly discovered. With what good faith these old books of barbarous men record the genesis of the world. Their best attempts to narrate how it is that star and earth and man exist, run out into some gigantic mythology, which, when it is ended, leaves the beautiful principal facts where they were, and the stupid gazing fabulist just as far from them as at first. Garrulity is our religion and philosophy. They wonder and are angry that some persons slight their books and prefer the thing itself. But with all progress this happens, that speech becomes less, and finally ceases in a noble silence" [Emerson and Emerson (vi: 274 - 75)].

Here is where we see Emerson (who reveres literature!) assert something that is unexpected but otherwise consistent with the rest of his thought and that we later amplify. His point is that literature is not a primary but a secondary enterprise, that reality itself is far more important than literature, and that all literature can hope to do is help us move closer to that reality, which ever remains beyond our grasp – like the utter hopelessness confronting God's servant, hapless Job, in attempting to perceive that which only God can understand. Thus, Emerson asserts that literature merely augments the work of the seer and priest. A still further but corroborating truth (and paradox) is that books themselves "are the destruction of literature. 'The golden age of the Greek literature was that in which no book grew under the stylus or the calamus, but these merely served as aids to the precarious tradition of the nature, and the overladen memory of the poetical singers and narrators"'[Emerson and Emerson (viii: 553)].[30] In the end, then, "Literature is a poor trick when it busies itself to make words pass for things" [Emerson and Emerson (V: 334)]. So writers must go sadly forward, recognizing their challenge of bringing into expression the insights gained from the Oversoul; secretly acknowledging the unavoidable failure (to them disaster!) that must attend their most earnest efforts; yet hoping to find within themselves the discipline to give birth to every unavoidably stunted expression.

c. <u>Day-to-Day Discipline</u>. Notwithstanding the above guarantee of ineffectual expression, the writer must follow through day to day and moment to moment with the conceived purpose without being side-tracked or distracted. This forward motion requires a concrete expression of will; the wisdom to accept imperfection in the attempt to create; and the persistence or discipline, nonetheless, to hold to the purpose that has been identified.

To be specific, writers exert this latent but flawed power of expression only when they possess the discipline actually to complete some design [Emerson and Emerson (ix: 54)], to bring to fruition the first impulse of the will; but to find such discipline and thus to complete such designs, the writer must be endowed with a remarkable persistence; and Emerson asserts brutally that only those so endowed are "of any account in Nature...." [Emerson and Emerson (ix: 217)] When such people can complete their work [Emerson and Emerson (viii: 518)], we call them classicists, meaning that they possess "the prerogative of a vigorous mind ... able to

---

[30] Emerson quotes from Letters by Barthold Georg Niebuhr (1776 - 1831), a prominent historian of German and Danish descent. He is perhaps best known for his study of ancient, especially Roman, history.

execute what [they conceive]" [Emerson and Emerson (ix: 25)], an ability involving simply starting a thing at the beginning and taking "all the steps in order" [Emerson and Emerson (viii: 539)], as "There are steps and limitations in the universe, and not a huddle of identity only" [Emerson and Emerson (vii: 37 - 38)]. For Emerson, the opposite of what he calls the "classic" procedure is the blunder of attempting "too many things," of permitting "unlimited activity," which guaranties "bankruptcy" or failure [Emerson and Emerson (viii: 516)]. Rather than "sprain" or "strain" themselves by attempting too much, writers should be content with the "temperate expression" of what they know; and under the influence of this prudence or moderation, they should sing only "for gods and demigods," "beget[ting] Messiahs" by "mere superfluity of … strength …." [Emerson and Emerson (viii: 418)] Stated differently, "T is very important in writing that you do not lose your presence of mind. Despair is no muse, and he who finds himself hurried, and gives up carrying his point this time, writes in vain" [Emerson and Emerson (ix: 175)]. Pythagoras seems the first to have spoken of the severity of this type of literary discipline, comparable to that demanded of a soldier. But sadly, literary discipline is so rare that the public has low expectations and does not bother to demand the required discipline from the writer [Emerson and Emerson (viii: 474)], whom, again, we must hold to as strict a law as we hold the pilot who loses his post because he swings "his vessel from the wharf with one intention, and after letting her go, changes his intention, and a vessel, deceived by his first demonstrations, is run affront of and injured...." [Emerson and Emerson (vii: 114)] For only "in the continuance, in fortitude, in working against pleasure, to the excellent end and conquering all opposition" does one go beyond knowledge and wisdom to achieve moral power, virtue, or completion, acquired only by enduring "routine and sweat and postponement of fancy to the achievement of a worthy end" [Emerson and Emerson (vii: 114-15)].

Thus, like skating, good writing requires "a subserviency to the will" [Emerson and Emerson (vii: 334)] which allows authors to adapt themselves to external circumstance and be able to produce under adverse conditions: "load as they go," "read as they run," and "write in a cab." They cannot, like "the heavy men," wait for the eagle to alight, for the swallow to roost like a barn fowl, for the river to run by, for the pause in the conversation, which never comes till the guests take their hats. Rarely can tame a wild horse, but can he make a wild a tame horse; it were better" [Emerson and Emerson (ix: 183-84)]. This all comes to mean that all effective performance presupposes a "fanaticism in the performer" [Emerson and Emerson (ix: 203)], an obedience to one's own genius that itself resembles a kind of religious faith [Emerson and Emerson (vi: 483)].

To be sure, writing seems too rare because it is, on the face of it, impossible – until it has actually been done [Emerson and Emerson (vi: 506)]. The truth is that the latter or "outward organization" is only "half"; for to create, or to produce this "outward organization," "it requires a will as perfectly organized." The perfect freedom which only the Will can bestow is the only force that can work, through Time, to counter the gravity or retrograde pull of Nature, which ruthlessly draws one away from the stars and back into one's head, rather than move one forward to build a vehicle that allows others to see what one has conceived. "When that Will is born, and ripened, and tried, and says, 'Here stand I, I cannot otherwise,' Nature surrenders as meekly as the ass on which Jesus rode. 'T is because the man is by much the larger half; and, though we exaggerate his tools and sciences, yet the moment we face a hero or a sage, the arts and civilizations are *peu de cas*" [Emerson and Emerson (ix: 21)]. In short, as regards the need for discipline, writers should hold to their purpose "with the tough impracticality of gravitation itself" [Emerson and Emerson (viii: 217)]; for only then can they subdue this gravity, this inherent inertia, and rise to command what they create.

In other words, by way of summarizing the above theory of expression, not only must writers be "up to Nature and the First Cause in [their] consciousness" of the Oversoul, but they also must be able "to collect and swing [their] whole vital energy into one act, and leave the product there for the despair of posterity...." [Emerson and Emerson (vii: 277)] The fact that this executive power is possessed in degrees explains, still again, why "a day is one thing to Shakespeare and another to John A. Coomb" [Emerson and Emerson (ix: 536)].[31]

2. The Writer's Imaginative Capacity and the Literary Womb. As writers move forward to demonstrate the ability to guide the form through future stages of expression, it gradually dawns upon them that this effort of expression can go no further unless they learn to take the insight which they have literally wrested from the Oversoul like Hercules, and build upon or expand this perception. It may be argued that this recognition is analogous to a mother's first inkling of pregnancy, although this analogy breaks down when we realize that the mother has, supposedly, no conscious ability to mold or direct the zygote, as does the writer. Nonetheless, I am forced to use this trope of

---

[31] John A. Coomb is a possibly fictional character for whom, at Coomb's supposed request at a gathering, Shakespeare invented an hilarious epitaph: "Ten in the hundred lies here engrav'd,/Tis a hundred to ten his soul is not sav'd;/If any man ask, 'Who lies in this tomb?'/Oh! Oh! quoth the Devil, 'tis my John A. Coomb."

conception as the best way of intimating what must be taking place, even unconsciously, in the mind of a would-be writer. In their heads writers are becoming aware of a building process brought about through the use of the imagination. In the projection of creative work, such expansion would have to come from the imagination; for what else can be its source, as creation necessarily involves projecting the mind into the future of the object about to be created? This new movement suggests that anything created begins in and is protected by a mental womb. Here is to be nourished the "zygote" that the Oversoul has helped to supply to the writer. But this spark must next build, transform, or expand itself into a fuller idea or concept (the "embryo") before it can exist outside of the womb as a living entity (or "infant"). In this process of development, the entity to be created demonstrates a three-fold nature, merely replicating the triplicities that one constantly sees throughout Nature. This entity is first a zygote, then an embryo, and finally a viable infant (imprinted with the script or code needed to enable its further development outside of the womb).

a. Imagination and the Literary Womb. The writer must employ the imagination to develop the zygote into the embryo and then into the infant. By virtue of working only in a parallel or secondary universe, the writer must fall back upon the notion of correspondence. In this universe, everything corresponds to, has reference to, but is not in itself, Nature. The writer is forced to work in a mental womb, shell, or echo chamber in which everything created is analogical, symbolic, or metaphoric. Everything becomes a pattern of, for, or to, something else, and this something else is Nature. The writer is, we might say, confined within a golden or enchanted egg, and everything within its circumference is thereby enchanted

To construct this universe, the writer must first exercise the power actually to build forms, not randomly, but guided by the discipline of imitating consciously or unconsciously, methods laid out in Nature. However, though Nature is primary, and the parallel world of literature is at best secondary, Nature does put in the writer's hands a special, non-material tool, which is primarily the writer's image or conceptualization of Nature. Even though Emerson laments that the somewhat superficial relationship to Nature established through language is ultimately disappointing, because it soon dawns upon the writer that the work cannot directly touch Nature but is merely a way of approximating it, there is also in the inevitability of this type of failure a definite and very powerful creative opportunity – one might say, compensation. Humanity can still learn from these language-based approximations, which are nothing more than abstractions or extractions or extrapolations of human cognitions of, from, and about Nature. In Kantian terms, these extrapolations are "phenomena" (the distorted perceptions of Nature, passed through the prism of the writer' consciousness) but never "noumena" or the thing-in-itself.

Yet, for the writer, these imprecise concepts render Nature in a certain respect pliant and useable where otherwise it would be inaccessible. Though there are ways that some humans can affect and even mold Nature itself (consider the chemist, who can affect the composition of matter; the engineer, who can construct tangible structures from matter; or the doctor, who can change the matter of the human form from a state of sickness to wellness), these capabilities are not within the reach of the writer-artist – nor should they be. But what the writer can do is manipulate the image of Nature and use the imagination to bend at least this image to artistic ends, which ends are never in any case material. The writer seeks to affect the mind and emotions of the audience but not its flesh. In their own right, and through their secondary or mental methods, writers become molders or vitalizers of a kind of "inner" Nature [Emerson and Emerson (viii: 254)], without which capacity Nature for them would remain a brute and alien effect, but through the aid of which the images from and about Nature become a linguistic code, in and of itself [Emerson and Emerson (X: 459-60)] – the only code, in fact, which writers have at their disposal and with which they continually struggle. Writers eventually conclude that they never can possess or understand matter unless they grasp it as this linguistic, non-physical, representation [Emerson and Emerson (viii: 572)].

Emerson goes a step further to assert that, just as matter is otherwise meaningless for humanity (for writers) if not informed or made use of on the level of thought, so "a thought which does not go to embody or externalize itself, is no thought," and hence is likewise useless to humans. This seems to mean that just as writers need the images of Nature to externalize thought, so no thought would be meaningful or accessible to them unless it could be concretized and made intelligible by imagery from Nature [Emerson and Emerson (ix: 175)].[32] Thus, when writers express themselves about pliant matter by using concepts, as they must, they acquire a unique power, which presumably allows them at least to control their second-hand perception of Nature, though not (as, again, is obvious) Nature Itself. In this way, the representation of Nature can become a definitive language, though this language is just as destined as regular, linguistic

---

[32] We are here referring to what Emerson says in his book *Nature* about how matter is empty for man unless married to thought.

utterance, to remain "opaque," "transparent," "fluent" with no "solid bottom," or a "bubble." Still, according to Emerson, the artist's vivified, though imprecise, form allows a degree of light from heaven to pass through to us as receptors.

There can and must exist, therefore, a choreographed dance between the writer's perceptions of Nature and Nature Itself by which the imagination can establish over all a kind of mental control or guidance. This, after all, remains the central problem of the writer, as we have suggested. The consciousness of the writer becomes the necessary prism through which the Oversoul can shine and by which a nascent zygote can grow. Through this control, the writer can weave isolated perceptions of Nature into coordinated concepts [Emerson and Emerson (viii: 504)]. Indeed, a single "thought, any thought, pressed, followed, opened, dwarfs nature, custom, and all but itself" [Emerson and Emerson (x: 166)]. Matter then can become a symbol, a representative or "an exponent of some general principle or law." Stated differently, the mind of the writer can find the approximate thought [Emerson and Emerson (viii: 536)], and Nature supplies the "words to clothe" that thought.[33]

But the writer uses the Mind to establish not only a vertical connection from mind to perceived fact or image in Nature, but also a horizontal connection among these thought-governed images. Through the right use and placement of such images [Emerson and Emerson (ix: 547)] once controlled in these ways by the writer, the world and all in it invariably become the school or university for the author [Emerson and Emerson (x: 64)], and the zygote in this imagined or parallel world is at last subject to the writer's will and ready to move forward to become a developing embryo.

---

[33] This is, again, a central point of *Nature*.

b. <u>Imagination and the Principle of Progression</u>. Although writers must use the imagination to develop the embryo in the womb, they encounter a fundamental Emersonian crisis. I speak of Emerson's often-referred-to distinction between the creations of talent and the creations of genius. To strictly preserve the analogy between the embryo and the creative production of the writer at this stage, we will have to consider that, just as there can be born individuals that are mediocre in gifts (which Emerson tends to call "talents"), so there are mediocre or merely imitative literary creations. Further, just as there are born individuals of great gifts (which Emerson calls "genius"), so there are exceptional and quite original literary creations. And we must remember that it is only the latter individual or genius which can communicate with the Oversoul to give Humanity something of real value, and Emerson is interested only in this type of individual or creation.

Imagination expands the metaphorical zygote into a metaphorical embryo under the law of progression. For even though what the writer creates in this analogical world can never match or exceed what Nature so elegantly produces, the would-be writer comes to realize that the next step forward must be guided by a seemingly universal and unavoidable law which presses everything in the universe into a state of unremitting development, change, and, ostensibly, progress. In doing so, the writer is contributing unawares to the sublime and mysterious activity of the Oversoul in creating the world; and it is this participatory activity directed by the Oversoul which seems to be the whole point and objective of divine communication with the human mind, in the first place. This notion of the writer's perhaps unwitting participation in some aspect of the divine creative process is fully consistent with Emerson's fundamental theories of each individual's supposedly special place and work in a constantly-evolving universe, just as this notion is consistent with the idea that the writer's universe is a mirror of or parallel to that of Nature.

Yet, to Emerson, this building capacity, this exercise of the will in the parallel world, must ultimately produce something not routine but original, for creation in and of itself is worthless. Why? Emerson seems to suggest that, just as the imagination is needed to build a parallel universe, so it is forced to participate in what appears to be a divine law and that only a new creation can be in line with God's ultimate Purpose. Of course, about this supposed Law of Originality we seem to have only limited knowledge, we have to be guided by our instinct in fulfilling it, and we can act only upon what we think we know.

Emerson admits that about this supposed Law of Originality he could say little, since none of us have "learned the law of the mind; nor can we control and bring at will or domesticate the high states of contemplation and continuous thought" [Emerson and Emerson (x: 129 - 30)]. To be exact, though we are admittedly ignorant of the "logic" which "put[s] us in training for the laws of creation" in and of themselves, we are even more unable to "describe how we can move forward from one species to a higher species of an existing genus. Yet, though the ass is not the parent of the horse and though no fish begets a bird, the concurrence of new conditions necessitates a new object in which those conditions meet and flower." This means that, when the hour is struck in onward nature, announcing that all is ready for the birds of higher form and nobler function, not one pair of parents, but the whole consenting system thrills, yearns, and produces. It is a favorable aspect of planets and of elements" [Emerson and Emerson (viii: 409-10)]. Emerson thus concludes that, in order to work along lines similar to those of God, the artist's purpose must be, to do, not what has already been done, but rather that which is new and yet somehow useful. The writer must accomplish "that undone something which is now hinting and working and impatient here in and around us" [Emerson and Emerson (vi: 360)].

When writers are unable to create according to this truth, they must perforce be imitators. They may, of course, build in the parallel universe, but what they build ensures mediocrity. Since only relative achievement can be the hope of artists, they can at least endeavor to fashion something new, and not choose this sickness of imitating other artists [Emerson and Emerson (viii: 453)]; for "[a]ll references to models, all comparison with neighboring abilities and reputations" guarantees mediocrity [Emerson and Emerson (vi: 520-21)], when mediocrity cannot possibly be the goal.

Here there arises what will seem a contradiction when we compare this sentiment later to a notion in Chapter 7, where we consider the idea that the new writer can benefit from the established canon of previous writers. This is, of course, a form of imitation or of modeling one's work after that of well-known authors, but this effort is merely a means to an end and is (or should be) educational in its intent. The end is to help the writer use models to find her or his own voice, not ultimately to mimic the voice of another. Yet, added to writers' primary frustration that they can produce only imperfection is the realization that something truly new comes only once in five hundred years" [Emerson and Emerson (vii: 520-21)]. Indeed, "[m]odern criticism is plainly coming to look on literature and arts as parts of history, that is, as growths," which can readily appear in time as well as disappear [Emerson and Emerson (viii: 322)]. These facts only intensify the suffering and insecurity of writers, and they are left with the intention of doing the best they can.

Emerson offers some insight into the reason that artists have been granted the power, and bear the responsibility, of producing something new in Nature, despite the fact that their creation is secondary to Nature's and is likely, at any rate, to fail. It may simply be that the artist is partaking of – indeed, aiding in the application of -- this divine law, whose alternate name may be the law of progress or even of evolution. Novelty always embodies the fact that we are creatures of transition, always in a state of metamorphosis from one condition to another: Nature steeps us "in the sea which girds the seven worlds, and makes us free of them all ....What we call the Universe today is only a symptom or omen of that to which we are passing. Every atom is on its way onward. The universe circulates in thought. Every thought is fleeting. Our power lies in transition...." [Emerson and Emerson (x: 457-48)] So fundamental in Nature is this impulse towards transition that the writer (and everyone who creates) is merely a vehicle by which this process can be expressed or implemented, such that the "good book grows whether the writer is awake or asleep; its subject and order are not chosen, but preappointed" [Emerson and Emerson (vii: 135)] – a notion that was advanced when we spoke earlier about the origin of subject matter. Originality involves, then, the writer's passing, not only "from thought to thought easily," but also "from realization to realization" [Emerson and Emerson (viii: 230)], an advance from a state of relative ignorance to one of greater knowledge or potency. Such discovery is made possible because, "Everything, by being, comes to see and to know. Work is eyes, and the [artists inform themselves] in efforming matter" [Emerson and Emerson (viii: 563)]. This principle of novelty in the production of literature is, once again, a law of Nature Itself, as one can see from the striking similarities between the goals of poet, gardener, and pomologist, all of whom have in common the task of invisibly guiding or overseeing incipient changes [Emerson and Emerson (vii: 313-14)]. Like the bee who produces honey from mint and marjoram or the chemist who transforms hydrogen and oxygen into water, "the poet listens to all conversations and receives all objects of Nature to give back, not them, but a new and perfect and radiant whole" [Emerson and Emerson (x: 236)]. Through such indefinable methods the very mathematician and materialist are forced to a similar poetic result, forced to acknowledge the inevitability, not of a stasis, but of a progressive metamorphosis, the fact that one ultimately must move forward or fall backward, must participate either in motion that is "progressive" or motion that is retrograde or characterized by "arrested development" [Emerson and Emerson (x: 236)]. This principle renders the unoriginal piece retrograde or at least static and the original piece forward looking, progressive, and therefore necessary. Thus, in this unavoidable change that characterizes Nature, Emerson seems to insist that there be also something new, expansive, or not before seen – something beyond the trite, hackneyed, mediocre, and expected, just as Aphrodite was an enticement surprising and new. Creative capacity presupposes that forms must evidence something totally new because the artist, too, is a creator (though inept) in Nature and consciously or unconsciously supports the overall evolutionary purpose of the Oversoul, whatever, in fact, that purpose may be. This means that the writer's appropriation of a portion of God's Will is expected and divinely ordained. We have said that literature is by nature analogical, in that words are not the Kantian thing-in-itself but merely *stand for* the thing-in-itself. Thus, the writer's work, being based in symbol, must employ the language of symbol. The construction of a new literary form leads eventually to the notion of the construction of new representative forms in the parallel world of thought; and these new representative forms are, in fact, literary embryos, developing from the embedded zygote.

c. <u>Imagination and the Encoded Blueprint</u>. Through imagination, also, the writer must supply some type of pre- or proto-form, some embryonic blueprint, from which later the actual physical structure of a work (the "infant") can emerge, in a post-natal activity designated as "composition." Besides creating the egg or parallel universe in which the writer must exclusively toil, the imagination has so far achieved two things. First, it has created the zygote or creative starting point, presumably embodying the impress of the Oversoul. Second, the imagination is responsible for not only expanding this seed, but also for making it hopefully original and hence "progressive." But the imagination is also needed to weave these two principles into an expressive blueprint or plan that will guide the infant after birth. This requires some explanation.

There is a difference between what is created and built up in the imagination and what is or can be executed, following imaginative activity. This difference is echoed by an earlier one when Emerson distinguishes between the eye that sees (the writer's contact with the Oversoul) and the hand that does (the writer's separate ability to create the vehicle that can express or communicate that vision). We are speaking, on the one hand, of the golden or enchanted egg, which is the parallel universe created by the imagination and, on the other hand, what happens after the egg is hatched, after the imagined creature is born. Linking these two states of the potential and the concrete, there must be a blueprint which encodes the general parameters of future expression by what we can refer to as "composition" proper.

Everyone would agree that, depending on the creative field (say, chemistry, philosophy, politics, religion), tangible or outer forms necessarily differ. Each participant in the Oversoul must perforce evidence a different personality, mode of expression, or form, so to speak. The analogy would be to the body of the embryo, which, before leaving the womb, retains within itself the capacity for a later growth, which we recognize as the growth from infancy to adulthood, and the code which the human embryo brings with it from the womb differs from that which, say, a bird embryo brings. What I am saying is that a proto or imagined blueprint created in the literary womb will characterize everything the literary embryo can become after birth. What we must grasp about this supposed encoding activity itself is that, differing from creative field to creative field, there is an overall encoding process, there is a variation of the process depending upon the nature of the creative field, and there is a literary version of this encoding phenomenon.

What is being described in the imaginative stage is a kind of gestation, analogous to the period of a life between conception and birth. Something happens interiorly in the womb as in the imagination of the writer which causes the zygote to grow before it receives or appropriates a body capable of surviving on its own in the world. For the writer, this gestation period involves, first, the coming to terms with the Emersonian paradox of the inherent failure of language to grasp the Kantian noumena and the acceptance of the need to use the mind to "control" Nature in the only way possible to the writer – by appropriating Nature as merely an image, a clothing, or a language for all that must be said. Once writers reach this stage, then they are admittedly secondary masters of Creation, while Nature is the primary master.

This gestation period, second, offers an opportunity to a new self, a unique and uncharted creation, a supposedly new life budding in the writer's mind which threatens one day to initiate something new in the minds of the waiting public, whom the writer by definition serves.

Third, the embryo takes form in the womb and draws upon the phylogeny or destined pattern which will make it recognizable as a particular type or ontogeny when it is born. This refers to the creation's taking shape in the metaphorical language characterizing literature. Certainly, this analogy between the gestation period of an infant and that of a literary work is inexact and perhaps unjustified, but the consideration of the analogy helps us to understand better what must be taking place (certainly unconsciously) in the imagination of the writer at this fragile, interior, but absolutely unavoidable stage between discovery of the subject matter based upon the writer's relation to the Oversoul and the time before the literary object acquires "body" – that is to say, a final, concrete form.

I cannot speculate about what this plan or blueprint might be for the non-writer. But we can ask, with Wordsworth, what distinguishes the blueprint created by a scientist, a philosopher, or a mathematician from the blueprint created by the writer? [Wordsworth et al.][34] But Wordsworth, in speaking about the very material (language) with which the poet's parallel universe is actually made, senses a difference between the mode of language expression employed by a scientist and that employed by a poet,

---

[34] Consider Wordsworth's famous explanation in the "Preface to the Lyrical Ballads."

and we will be forgiven the impudence of applying what he says to writing in general. Indeed, Wordsworth leads us to believe that the writer (in contrast to the scientist) employs a special language format characteristic of and indispensable to literature [Emerson and Emerson (x: 213)]. This is the difference between poetic and non-poetic language. For in this distinction of expression, the writer uniquely differentiates himself, not only from the scientist, but also from all of the other conduits of the Oversoul. Ostensibly, the perception and use of the Oversoul empowers the philosopher, the mathematician, the theologian, the musician, or the politician with different inherent codes. Here is where a distinction emerges between one type of recipient of the Oversoul and another type of recipient, as identified above when we spoke of those who are capable of being conduits of the Oversoul. All are potential conduits; but having said so, we have to think that their methodologies and means of expression must differ. Writers not only must ply their trade in the parallel universe of the imagination, but they must use a language, mode of expression, format, or inherent encoding that is appropriate and necessary to their particular universe. This is another way of asserting that the writer is compelled to flesh out the work by doubtless imitating what must have been the procedure that caused Aphrodite to be born from the foam of the sea – first, the water (Oversoul); second, the foam (Imagination): and third, the *potential* goddess (the literary code) – after which process the *actual* or compositional goddess is born.

What is this supposed literary code? The answer seems to be that in a literary creation there ought to be a three-fold expression: there should be an undeniable unity which holds together all of the parts of a piece; there should be an evenness or at least an abundance of development so that the form is adequate to the task of expression; and the language will be, more likely than not, more metaphorical, more universal, more morally instructive, more analogical, truer, and hence (at least for Wordsworth) more permanent than that of science. I am willing to believe that the first and second features of the literary code may also apply to creative production in all of the many fields influenced by the Oversoul. But I think that the third feature, if not unique to literature (the theologian, for instance, trades in symbol, analogy, and metaphor), is nonetheless characteristic of it, and that this is the truth that Wordsworth articulates, despite his insinuation (not really practiced by him) that literary language turns its back on the trope. Especially through this third feature, the author differentiates the blueprint used in science from that which will be literarily expressive and which thus becomes fully concretized in the impending demonstration of the writer's compositional skill.

The *first* encoding focuses on what is truly important in literature (though certainly not unique to it) – namely, unity or – as some may like to call it – synthesis. As stated above, writers' use of the Mind (vertically) to relate thought to facts and (horizontally) to connect thoughts to other thoughts extends to them the potential of exercising a godlike control over anything they may imaginatively create [Emerson and Emerson (ix: 547)]. This control is initially brought about when artists make only one potent thought the parent of their poem or other composition [Emerson and Emerson (x: 278)]. This specifically requires writers to search in their work for that one clue which can "bind" and unify [Emerson and Emerson (viii: 463)]. This process connotes "a steady respect to the whole by an eye loving beauty in details...," allowing writers to express "the One, or the Same, by the

Different" [Emerson and Emerson viii: 490)], just as on one level the same thought can be translated into scenery, animals, and human form and character and on a more universal level into several alternate languages, or into other "parallel mansions in God's house" -- drawing, sculpture, music, poetry, architecture [Emerson and Emerson (vii: 173-74; viii: 453)]. This single thought or unifying "interior impulse ... is the authentic mark of a new poem," "felt in the pervading tone, rather than in brilliant parts or lines; as if the sound of a bell, or a certain cadence expressed in a low whistle or booming, or humming, to which [poets] first timed [their] step, as [they] looked at the sunset, or thought, was the incipient form of the piece, and was regnant through the whole" [Emerson and Emerson (x: 267)].

Second, constructing the literary blueprint or encoding involves the ability of the writer, not only imaginatively to discover its unifying thread, but also to develop the piece by means of a related capacity of the imagination. In other words, the imagination must be widely-ranging, abundant, or diverse enough to allow writers to create from it some whole, rather than fragments [Emerson and Emerson (vi: 360)] – that is, to flesh out the piece evenly.[35] Emerson actually draws the surprising conclusion that this idea of abundant and intense imagination is what we mean when we speak of symmetry or proportion in a work [Emerson and Emerson (v: 437)]. At least one can concede that it is only through an abundant imagination that symmetry or proportion can ultimately be achieved. As suggested in the previous chapter concerning subject matter, art must have both a mental and material basis, or it will not be born. With respect to this

---

[35] This is obviously one of the defects of Samuel Taylor Coleridge's "Kubla Khan."

reciprocity between mind and matter [Emerson and Emerson (viii: 506-07)], the two together make possible the basic game of intellect, which is that all activity, all events, all states can be described or explained by means of a universal proposition and that these same universal or general propositions can be made "poetical again by being particularized" or embodied in some type of concretion [Emerson and Emerson viii: 382)]. Thus, development of a piece presupposes, not only "the power of invention, the freedom of thinking" [Emerson and Emerson (x: 195)], but also, it involves "Perception; Memory ...," "degrees of intellect," "which give birth to mythology" [Emerson and Emerson (viii: 568)] – a mythology that creates its own colorful universe out of the drab one in which we are forced to live. Indeed, "Original power in [writers] is usually accompanied with [such] assimilating power," which seems to operate under the illusion that the imagined is real. In this way, poets are able to string together worlds "like beads" upon their thought, and this imaginative ability can alone signify the genuineness, the originality, of the poet. For Shakespeare, the imagined object was so apparently powerful that it appeared before him as though it were real [Emerson and Emerson (viii: 520-21)]. It is this notion that there should be an even and abundant development of a piece which, for Emerson, accounts for the success of Shakespeare, whose intellect, rather than expressing itself in intervals, distributes itself evenly and unremittingly, across his entire work [Emerson and Emerson (x: 34-35)]. Indeed, an indefatigable imagination was one of Shakespeare's distinctive assets, as he "saw no better heaven or earth, but had the power and need to sing, and seized the dull ugly England ... and," through his imagination, "made it amicable and enviable to all reading [individuals]...." [Emerson and Emerson (viii: 507)]

Third, and more characteristically literary, not only does the encoding involve the finding of a unifying thread and the use of an abundant and proportionate imagination, but invariably (as is ultimately the point) literature connotes figurative, rather than literal or scientific language.[36] It is true that art which attempts to represent Nature photographically "is a miracle of delight to every eye"; but "ideal representation, which, by selection and much omission, and by adding something not in nature, but profoundly related to the subject, and so suggesting the heart of the thing, gives a higher delight, and shows an artist, a creator" [Emerson and Emerson (ix: 424-25)]. As writers interweave their concepts with their personal experience, they come to realize that what matters is not what happens in their lives, literally, but their ability to distinguish the essential from the non-essential experience and to report in their work on what is truly significant. This means that what is important in literature (here, Emerson says poetry) is not the actual "history" of the author's experience but its "music," not "fact" but "affection" -- music and affections' being ninety-nine percent of the whole story [Emerson and Emerson (vii: 318)]. It is for this reason that literature tends naturally towards figurative language – language which draws upon our inherent dependence upon and identity with Nature. One of the most important tools of literature is the figure of speech, especially metaphor or analogy, which, involving "identity of ratio," indicates the best in human perception. It expresses "our profound feeling of interest in the whole of nature. Everyone feels that everything is his cousin, that [she or he] has to do with all. Blot out any part of nature, and [one] too would lose" [Emerson and Emerson (viii: 271-72)]. Emerson characteristically asserts that we

---

[36] Think, again, of Wordsworth.

"will find the type (or the analogy or symbol), not only in kind, but in quantity, of all [our] moral and mental properties in the great world without ...." [Emerson and Emerson (viii: 217)] This suggests that metaphor fascinates us because we are even ourselves in essence nothing but a trope. Indeed, the ability to see the world figuratively or "representatively implies high gifts." Accordingly, poets like Shakespeare use objects, not according to their right name "in the sphere of sense," but "representatively for those interior facts which they signify," for their symbolizing music [Emerson and Emerson (X: 262)]. Shakespeare created "by incessant surprises, [working] the miracle of mythologizing every fact of the common life; as snow, or moonlight, or the level rays of sunshine," thereby lending "a momentary glory to every pump and woodpile" [Emerson and Emerson (x: 27)].

3. <u>The Writer's Compositional Skill</u>. In the above section, "The Writer's Imaginative Capacity," we discussed in general the activity of the imagination in creating, expanding, and encoding in an enchanted universe, but we will pursue an extension of this topic in detail in this section, "The Writer's Compositional Skill." This so-called compositional skill refers to how the writer manipulates or brings into manifestation this literary coding or blueprint. Here, we are reminded of the Latin root of this term "composition" (*componere*), meaning to put together or to assemble from disparate parts, but what this definition implies is that these disparate parts can be "assembled" only if there is a plan, blueprint, or coding that guides this activity. In fact, the piece takes an additional step forward into concretion through its ability to clothe this so-far imagined and emerging vehicle with

some type of final or concrete literary form, again according to an inherent literary blueprint. This procedure, though discussed above in its interior or "natal" aspect (the birthing analogy seems inevitable), requires much amplification when speaking about what happens when the delicately developing embryo emerges from the womb as an infant endowed with the capacity of growth and hence gifted with a new future. We are speaking of turning the imagined literary *potential* into an *actuality* that can be published, that is to say, made accessible to an interested public. This culminating phase of form construction involves three things: giving the object a final or dispositive design as guided by the blueprint; fleshing out that design, associated with the previous notion of constructing something new and progressive in the parallel universe; and ensuring its refinement as a form, related to the notion of the surface shell or blueprint derived from the interior, imagined, or golden egg.

Thus, in a peculiar sense, this third or compositional procedure not only is the culmination of the previous two processes (executive and imaginative) but oddly recapitulates or repeats analogous activities of these preceding interior stages: for imposing a design is reminiscent of our discussion of executive ability; fleshing out the object echoes the notion of imaginative building or expansion; and artistic refinement recalls the idea of analogical or metaphorical expression. One could even argue that the identified code of unity, adequacy, and analogic expression, or a pattern like it, is implied in each of the compositional processes, below; but I admit that these assumed connections have not been worked out meticulously by me. However interesting these echoes may be, the important point here is that the creative object is entering a climaxing stage. This final phase of construction is perhaps what Plato means when he

81

speaks of the physical chair as merely the shadow of the realer chair that exists on the plane of mind. If this phase is not handled as intelligently and as conscientiously as the executive and imaginative phases had to be handled, the infant may well enter the world deformed, if not still-born.

a. <u>Imposing an Appropriate Design</u>. To Emerson, what matters most in this final stage of construction is the development of a controlling design, which, he believes, is natural to all serious art and which should be the primary element that guides final execution, even though the design will vary according to the subject and occasion. And in this notion of design, one would also have to say, in connection with modernist and post-modernist work, that fragmentation or the supposedly conscious eschewing of a fixed design is likewise a species of design. But it is also important to keep in mind that the preliminaries of the design have been laid out or worked out in the previously described arena of the imagination. This activity is the subjective twin of what comes out to be the plan which the constructing mind, in due course, will grasp. This blueprint, plan, or code is the subjective plan or the design per se, that will govern the phase now under discussion.

As one might expect, Emerson observes that the same "good" art and architecture which we see in the solar system is also in the brain of the artist, if only she or he could be kept from making blunders [Emerson and Emerson (vii: 98)]. In some sense, this observation contradicts that made earlier when Emerson concludes that the work of the artist in imitating Nature must always fall short of the goal – indeed, must inevitably fail. But in this comment about mistakes, Emerson also does admit to the notion of a relative perfection. Thus, judging from Emerson's idea that the design that is in Nature is also in the brain of the artist, serious art must at least embrace some kind of design (even if, presumably, that decision about design is to have a modernist or fluid one), because – according to Emerson – the "architectural" impulse supposedly inherent to human nature, leads the writer always to precipitate "the particles held in solution by ... thought into a form which obeys and represents the thought" [Emerson and Emerson (x: 192)]. Hence, for Emerson, the issue of design, as an aspect of creativity in the arts, can never be overlooked, as design is the central way the artist has of imitating Nature.

The second that this rudimentary or inherent design emerges from the potential of the materials, then writers find themselves at the all-important "casting moment" [Emerson and Emerson (vi: 94)]; and the more definite the design which results from this casting moment, the more is the writer's purpose open to being appropriately adjusted, not only to produce the desired synthesis among the parts, but also to guide the work to its completion. Of course, the first question in this guidance concerns the purpose of the design and whether it is the spiritual mission of the author to complete the task [Emerson and Emerson (ix: 528)]. What is next important is that this design give meaning to the individual stones which make up the completed building. A single thought may appear valueless. But as soon as greater thought and broader scope suggest the "foregoers and followers" of this solitary idea, the worth of this single thought is greatly enhanced [Emerson and Emerson (x: 219)]; and (as we have seen above when Emerson discussed the building of the thought form in imagination) the building process involves, not only the unifying thought that creates coherence throughout, but also the ability of this single thought to connect adjacent facts. The latter aspect involves relating fact to fact; and the former, synthesizing all facts into one whole. Similarly, in collective arts like engineering or architecture, such as in the building of the system of locomotives, design even dwarfs the people who help to finish the grand project, making their achievement seem, not human, but godlike [Emerson and Emerson (ix: 301)]. Since human life of 70 years seems so short and since it takes so much time to achieve even these relatively insignificant effects, architecture is a particularly melancholy profession; for, in Emerson's words, "The time that is proper to spend in mere musing is too large a fraction of threescore years and ten to be indulged to [any] greatness of behavior."

Besides allowing the artist to make necessary adjustments which relate facts to facts and which promote synthesis, design provides the intellectual scaffolding by which the parts are organized or expressed. This particular power of design is to be valued above any other surface skill. In fact, art is nothing but a good design expressed by right details – which is why art is destroyed when the design is gaudily set aside; for "Then begins shallowness of effect; intellectual bankruptcy of the artist. All goes wrong; artist and public corrupt each other." Under these circumstances, scholars lose the very heart of their talent [Emerson and Emerson (ix: 528)]. The practical value of design as scaffolding is therefore obvious. In fact, design remains the chief tool of both the neophyte and the master, though their attitudes towards disclosing that design may differ, the beginning poet or craftsman's feeling that disclosure of the design will diminish his powers [Emerson and Emerson (vi: 368)], whereas a master like Hawthorne[37] may think so little about disclosing his design as

---

[37] Hawthorne, Nathaniel (1804 - 1864). American Romantic novelist and author of *The Scarlet Letter*.

indiscriminately to open the process to his public [Emerson and Emerson (vii: 188)]. Perhaps this practical value of design is indicated by the fact that, to lay people, the production of an object like a penknife, thimble, or pin seems so complicated, until they actually visit the shop or factory where it is made in its successive stages or parts. Design has made the construction so simple that they then devalue the object [Emerson and Emerson (vii: 262)]. Since, to Emerson, it is the function of art to inspire or elevate, the most important thing is that the design of a work suggest the existence of "a vast wealth, ... background, [or]... divinity." To this end, the ancients and subsequent great poets "elaborated their design, but slighted their finish," realizing that, "if this religion is in the poetry, it raises us to some purpose, and we can well afford some staidness or gravity in the verses" [Emerson and Emerson (viii: 532-33)].

Thus, design is not only inherent in us (and therefore inevitable) but also it is without doubt the most powerful construction tool at the writer's disposal, in that the development of a design forces writers continuously to recall their purpose; confers upon them a means by which they can bring their work under a type of unity, synthesis, or control; and puts into their hands a mechanism by which they can impose a type of intellectual scaffolding, by means of which they can more easily complete their plan.

Even if we assume that the impulse towards design is inherent and that it is essential in guiding the outward form of the project, writers need to learn the additional skill of adjusting these designs to subject matter and occasion even while being purposeful. Despite its immense diversity, Nature is itself purposeful in building the form of a tree or animal [Emerson and

Emerson (ix: 323)]. By the same token, so long as they are purposeful, writers may construct their own forms using any style, from the classical to the gothic to the post-modern [Emerson and Emerson vii: 247)]. This purposefulness presupposes that writers are masters of their craft and that, in the face of diversity of aims, can "carry [their] own end triumphantly through the most difficult" circumstance [Emerson and Emerson (ix: 8)].

The need for such versatility is especially apparent in literature; for in this medium, there are broad needs – ranging from extempore speaking to written discourses [Emerson and Emerson (v: 236)]; for we may be called upon to "write as variously as we dress and think." No forms better illustrate this range than the lecture, the novel, and the poem. Naturally the most uncomplicated of the three, the *lecture* ignores tradition and circumstance to speak sincerely to an audience on equal terms [Emerson and Emerson (v: 233-34)], using a few reasonable words to penetrate beyond appearance [Emerson and Emerson (vii: 82)], and endeavors, according to Emerson's quoting of Socrates,[38] "'To make the great, little, and the little, great....'"[Emerson and Emerson (vii: 67)] However, the *novel* is inevitably more complex, in that the novelist must manipulate the dual forces of faith and fate – the former by examining the hopes and feelings of protagonists and the latter by acknowledging a chain of events which condition the characters' internal impulses and block the realization of these impulses [Emerson and Emerson (viii: 500-01)].

On the other hand, *poetry* enjoys a freedom and flexibility light years beyond those of both the lecture and the novel, and it is easy to say that, though poetry also requires design, this feature must vary from poem to poem and (the well-known poetic

---

[38] Socrates (470BC – 399BC). Highly influential Greek philosopher and teacher of Plato.

genres, notwithstanding) must be left fully and uniquely to the individual poet. It is hardly surprising, then, that Emerson has much more to say about the poem, regarding it as the most challenging of the genres: because poetry seeks to express, not eminent, but supereminent experience; it is open in subject matter; and it is unpredictable in design.

Supereminent Experience. While the lecture or the novel may select the "eminent experiences," poetry isolates "the supereminent" [Emerson and Emerson (vii: 100)]. Because of such ability, Emerson (harkening back to the "Poetics" of Aristotle)[39] regards poetry as "more philosophical and excellent than history" [Emerson and Emerson (ix: 296)]; he considers philosophers, as "poetes manques, ... neutral or imperfect poets" [Emerson and Emerson (vii: 100)], or (as Thoreau[40] puts it) "broken down poets"; and "the broadest philosophy[, as] narrower than the worst poetry" [Emerson and Emerson (vii: 99)].

Open Subject Matter. In seeking the preeminent over the eminent experiences, poetry functions like the mind [Emerson and Emerson (x: 364)] or a unifier, correlating the most diverse types of people [Emerson and Emerson (x: 358 - 59)] and "detecting identity" beneath "the slightest change of name" or "under variety of surface" [Emerson and Emerson (viii: 296)], and this correlating activity creates in the consciousness of the reader "a new nomenclature" [Emerson and Emerson (v: 240)]. As a unifier, correlator, or affirmer, poetry resembles prayer [Emerson and Emerson (vi: 126; vi: 209)], and

---

[39] "Poetics." Aristotle's Treatise on Drama and Literary Theory. Aristotle (385 BC – 323 BC) was a premier Greek Philosopher and Student of Plato.
[40] Thoreau, Henry David (1817 - 1862). American philosopher and second only to Emerson as an exponent of the Transcendental movement. He is especially known as the author of *Walden Pond* and his essay "On the Duty of Civil Disobedience."

through its ability to affirm, poetry loses no time or opportunity for growth [Emerson and Emerson (x: 171)]; but like gravity, which holds the Universe together, and none knows what it is" [Emerson and Emerson (x: 436)], poetry involves "love and wonder and the delight in suddenly seen analogy" [Emerson and Emerson (ix: 182)]. This analogical lens, the foundation of all literature and especially the basis of poetry, connotes a simplicity of attitude that is more important than skill of execution. It is this simplicity which allows the poet to speak on any subject -- whether finance, manufacture, sunsets, or souls. So long as these subjects are treated in their true, rather than "kitchen" order, they are poetic; and thus, for the poet, every topic has abundant possibilities [Emerson and Emerson (vii: 229)]. Indeed, only the poet can teach the real political economy [Emerson and Emerson (viii: 389)].

Unpredictable Design. Although poetry searches out the sublime and has at its heart a simplicity of attitude, its form tends towards a concatenation of natural facts. Because of this concatenation, the design of a poem is frequently unpredictable. By virtue of its nature, whether we consider the poetry occasional (and hence giving a special opportunity for originality) [Emerson and Emerson (ix: 356)] or driven by a less transient purpose – poetry exhibits no laws, no rules, and no natural history but "is miraculous at all points" [Emerson and Emerson (vii: 296)], "new and incalculable" -- simultaneously, "as new as foam, and as old as the rock" [Emerson and Emerson (vii: 36)]. Though prose also requires "concatenation, a mass of facts, and a method," poetry is made possible through the mere emphasis upon Nature and through "the mere enumeration of natural objects" [Emerson and Emerson (ix: 561)]. Indeed, whereas in prose the referential function of the word seems dominant, words in poetry acquire qualities akin to the coloring and tonal nuances in painting and music [Emerson and Emerson.: ix: 413)]. Hence, in poetry connotation is just as important as, if not more important than, denotation. Emerson concludes that faults of language, growing from this referential tendency, show up more readily in poetry than in prose [Emerson and Emerson (ix: 14)], unless each poem is "made up of lines that are [themselves] poems" [Emerson and Emerson viii: 445, 523)]. In the end, the poem is made up of lines each of which filled the sky of the poet in its turn; for that reason, a true poem by no means yields all its virtue at the first reading, but is best when we have slowly and by repeated attention felt the truth of all the details" [Emerson and Emerson (x: 464)].

Even if design is inherent to us as creators, therefore, and even if it is indispensable to the production of a finished vehicle, writers must be capable of great flexibility in drawing upon this fundamental tool of construction. As a matter of fact, their potential as masters of their craft depends upon their flexibility as artistic designers. They must be capable of adapting their design to any purpose, circumstance, or audience. Emerson places great emphasis upon design because, without this kind of pre-ordering of their work, writers can never hope to complete a credible literary object.

b. <u>Fleshing Out or Developing the Design</u>. The work can expand meaningfully beyond the above mere design, only when writers themselves develop the design into a fleshed-out creature, just as earlier they expanded the content of their thought form through the use of the imagination. For Emerson, this development can be said to grow or to be made possible by three personal characteristics of the writer – namely, instinct, character, and (for lack of a better term) voice (which amounts to the writer's distinctive style). This notion of connecting the fleshing out process to the personality of the writer seems repulsive to the avid theorist, who would rather think that the process is more, let us say, "objective"! We have to assert, however, that this resistance on the part of the theorist is begging the question, since every stage has been and has to be related to the writer's personality in one way or another -- from the challenges of leisure which must be faced early on, to the issue of inspiration which is affected by the writer's personal lens, to the onerous mental and imaginative task of giving body at various stages to a particular work. It might even be suggested that the personality of the writer (whoever the writer is in flesh) will have some influence even during the phase of post-production, when the work is sent out to a public; for Emerson, as we will point out later, will suggest that those qualities which the writer has embodied in the work (through the prism, we have said, of the personality) can influence who will be attracted to the work and therefore, who will not only read the work, but also preserve what has been created. Further, it is because it has been processed through the furnace of the personality that the work carries with it, its (for Emerson) most important feature – that of moral and spiritual instruction, instruction which is meant, eventually, to "guide" the personalities, the lives, of the audience. At any rate, it is almost impossible to proceed in this discussion without relying on such flawed or inadequate terms as instinct, integrity, and voice.

First and foremost, in fleshing out a vehicle, the writer should rely upon her or his *instinct*, because only through this means does the work acquire its fundamental vitality or warmth. This instinct fires the writer, producing "[g]uidance and determination to an aim" that are not "mechanical" but "a placing" or "a polarity" [Emerson and Emerson (vii: 99)] that makes the writer a "fanatic" of the subject; and this fanaticism becomes a "fibre" reaching from the writer's heart to the subject, so that feeling and thought "can freely play" [Emerson and Emerson (ix: 207)].

This instinctual connection guides the writer quickly to the heart of a subject. When energy flows from writers' hearts to their subject, they can concentrate on the essentials rather than nonessentials and maintain "a just perception of what is important...." [Emerson and Emerson (x: 335)] Emerson observes that whenever he himself composes out of this warmth of connection, he can find ample wisdom, thoughts, and words; and that, at such times, he reads his paper "with the pleasure of one who receives a letter." However, whenever he writes without this ray of warmth or as a mere filler, the outcome "is hard and cold, is grammar and logic" without magic; and he does not want to reread it [Emerson and Emerson (v: 469)]. This absence of "animal heat" produces a "fatal frost," which renders the work "cheerless and undesirable," causing the reader to yawn, even if the product be elegant [Emerson and Emerson (viii: 40)].[41] This instinctual connection is, therefore, more important than refinement of form. Given the necessity of this connection, it "is better to be poor and helpless in doing, because our heart is preoccupied and astonished with the immensities of God, than to be at leisure to adorn and finish our trivial works because communication with the Deity is no longer open to us." To do so denigrates the place of "vision and union" in literature and elevates beyond their rightful station "the muses," whom the sages depicted only as

---

[41] The reader might compare these views with William Hazlitt's notion of gusto and Gertrude Stein's concept of passion.

"the daughters of memory," a faculty which must be dispelled, when true inspiration arrives [Emerson and Emerson (v: 511)]. This notion of establishing an instinctual connection with the vehicle being created seems to be Emerson's way of declaring that a writer must enjoy some sort of personal link to the subject matter and not attempt to write from abstractions; and this notion parallels, perhaps, the advice constantly meted out to beginning writers, to write from "their own experience," to stick to "what they know." Emerson asserts that without this purely personal connection, the work would be "lifeless."

The work should not only have an instinctual or personally energized mooring, but also it should somehow find expression through the personal *integrity* of the writer. This level of expression seems to lay the basis for the work's psychological or moral depth, as well as, as a parallel, its psychological and moral appeal to a future audience. Presumably, when authors evidence integrity, their works are more likely to be trusted and/or intellectually substantive than would be the case were these writers themselves shallow or dishonest [Emerson and Emerson (v: 506)]. In fact, when the writer stands by character rather than party, interest, or vanity, he "discovers that the first thought is related to all thought and carries power and fate in its womb" [Emerson and Emerson (ix: 247)]. Emerson ever points out that "talent," without this foundation in character, "is friskiness" [Emerson and Emerson (ix: 357)]. Emerson implies that such "friskiness" accounts for "modern antiques" like Martin Savage Landor's *Pericles and Aspasia*, or Johann Wolfgang von Goethe's *Iphigenia in Tauris*, or Christoph Martin Wieland's *The History of the Abderites,* or Samuel Taylor Coleridge's *The Rime of the Ancient Mariner*, or

Sir Walter Scott's *Lay of the Last Minstrel*,[42] which Emerson calls "paste jewels," that lack "verity and by which no one "will live or die" [Emerson and Emerson (vi: 400)]. Emerson seems to have formed a similar opinion even of Goethe's *Faust*, which he finds "a little too modern and intelligible," able to be manufactured "at several mills" [Emerson and Emerson (viii: 245)].

To Emerson, that the integrity or personal depth of the artist comes thus through in the work is evidenced by the moral power of Shakespeare [Emerson and Emerson (vi: 83-4)]. We have to believe that a person of substance was behind the work of Shakespeare, to whom "alone God granted the power to dispense with the humours of his company; they must needs all take his. He is always good, and Goethe knew it and said, 'It is as idle to compare Tieck to me as me to Shakespeare'" [Emerson and Emerson (viii: 245)].[43] In fact, so intellectually and morally formidable was Shakespeare that you could give your "rubbish" to him, and he would return it "in gold and stars," "illuminat[ing] every low or trite word," making each poetic by rendering it with a "higher thought" [Emerson and Emerson (ix: 540 - 41)].

Again, just as it is important that writers draw upon their own experience, instinct, and emotions rather than write from empty abstractions, so it is critical that they demonstrate integrity in producing the work. And of course, this is not a foreign notion at all; for we expect from writers a certain amount of honesty and

---

[42] Landor, Martin Savage (1775 - 1864). British Romantic poet and political activist. -- Wieland, Christoph Martin (1733 - 1813). German Enlightenment poet and writer. -- Coleridge, Samuel Taylor (1772 - 1834). Poet, Literary Critic, and One of the Founders of the Romantic Movement in England. -- Scott, Sir Walter (1771 - 1832). Scottish novelist known for historical romances like *Ivanhoe*.

[43] Tieck, Johann Ludwig (1773 - 1853). German writer, translator, and exponent of the Romantic movement.

sincerity of purpose, before we are willing to trust or give credence to their perceptions about anything.

The design is sequentially fleshed out, we have said, when Nature speaks initially through the instinct and later the integrity of the writer, keeping in mind that we fall back on this notion of sequence just for the sake of description and that these modes of fleshing out must certainly be simultaneous and intertwined. But the consummation of this sequence is achieved when the design is brought to fruition by the kind of vital language, or *voice*, that will capture (and hold) the attention of the public. We have to pause here, to recollect where we are in the creative cycle, because by this time, we have a perception from the Oversoul, and we have a blueprint formed in the imagination. We have also writers drawing from their own experience and writing from the depth of their sincerity. What we have immediately before us now, is the question of the specific language to be used, the screen or mirror into which the reader must peer. It is the actual language on the page, and, for Emerson, the key to this type of final language is always simplicity. This is by way of summary. But the thought of simplicity can be conveyed differently, can be "unpacked" (as some would describe the process) by asserting that the distinctive voice of the writer must be steeped in a special language. Specifically, this language must communicate in a manner that is authentic, accessible, and magnetic. Do we not see again the familiar triplicity and the tendency to echo previous triplicities? In short, the instinct and integrity mentioned above are not the only factors which affect the filling in or fleshing out of the literary vehicle, prior to its ultimate refinement for publication. The first two qualities are fundamental in Emerson's Transcendental philosophy; however, Emerson often elaborates on the latter quality of voice because of his enduring fascination for the art of rhetoric consistent with the Greco-Roman reverence for it. In Emerson's mind, the serious writer must also be concerned with this quality of "voice"; that is to say, with the art of communication or expression: "Wooden minds, wooden voices [Emerson and Emerson (x: 45)]. "Le style, c'est l'homme, said Buffon; and Goethe said, that, as for poetry, etc., he had learned to speak German; and I say of Burrill's fifty languages, that I shall be glad if he knows one; for if I be asked how many masters of English idiom I know, I shall be pestered to count three or four among living men" [Emerson and Emerson (viii: 489-90)].[44] This art of communication can be approximated when writers build into their expression at least three qualities – naturalness or authenticity, which is a spiritual characteristic which Emerson always extols; accessibility, which democratizes the literary object; and evocative appeal, which makes the piece magnetic or emotionally appealing. It must be noted that this question of expression is not so easy to understand or explain, in that it does "get down into the weeds" of composition and hence is variable, arbitrary, and often inaccessible to useful judgments. For this reason, we cannot help recalling the admonishments of Alexander Pope,[45] who simultaneously supported and inveighed against the following of mere "rules" of expression in composition.

---

[44] Buffon or Georges-Louis Leclerc, Comte de Buffon (1707 - 1788). French intellectual, mathematician, naturalist, and author of *Discours sur le Style* (1753), from which this assertion regarding style is taken. -- Burrill. This is very likely a reference to one Elihu Burritt (1810-1879), who was said to have been a master of fifty languages.

[45] Pope, Alexander (1688 – 1744). British writer, satirist, and the most prolific (and most quoted) of the neoclassical poets.

First and foremost, effective language must be *natural or authentic*, that is, rooted in Nature, because only this kind of language is fitted to convey the truth, which should be the aim of all of the writer's endeavors. Although Emerson regards the language of a piece as nothing more than "rhetoric" [Emerson and Emerson (x: 361)], the true "school of oratory" must be this truth [Emerson and Emerson (ix: 247)] "[T]he grace of God" must be the source of this rhetoric [Emerson and Emerson (x: 361)]. As such, Nature is the ultimate teacher of rhetoric: "She can teach thee, not only to speak truth, but to speak it truly ...." In most compositions, as Emerson reminded us in our discussion of the role of instinct in composition (and elsewhere), there is often one thought which was spontaneous, and many "which were added and abutted; but, in the true, God writes every word" [Emerson and Emerson (v: 444 - 45)], requiring of writers, thereby, that their work exhibit "nothing muddy or turbid, but shall be transparent, sublime as God pleases, but not eccentric" [Emerson and Emerson (vi: 83-4)]. William Cullen Bryant,[46] for instance, experienced Nature at first hand with directness and vividness, whereas young, contemporary poets, Emerson believed, worked only from pictures of Nature [Emerson and Emerson (x: 76-77: x: 80-82)].

When its rhetoric is rooted in Nature, the piece, exhibiting the "vital authority" of Islamic and Old Testament sermons [Emerson and Emerson (vii: 110-11)], acquires the type of eloquence "that shoves usurpers from their thrones, and sits down on them by allowance and acclaim of all" [Emerson and Emerson (ix: 276)]. This notion that rhetoric must be rooted in Nature is thus so vivid to Emerson that he constantly, and characteristically, employs figures of speech from Nature to describe either poetry or writing

---

[46] Bryant, William Cullen (1794 – 1878). American Romantic Poet.

in general, requiring that these arts resemble "the waves of Lake Michigan toss[ing] in the bleak snowstorm" [Emerson and Emerson (ix: 12)]; "the settlement of dew on the leaf, of stalactites on the wall of the grotto, the deposit of flesh from the blood, of woody fibre in the tree from the sap" [Emerson and Emerson (V: 512)]; or "hickory nuts, so fresh and sound." Emerson says, "[when I observe] the sweeping sleet amid the pine woods, my sentences look very contemptible, and I think I will never write more: but the words prompted by an irresistible charity, the words whose path from the heart to the lips I cannot follow, are fairer than the snow" [Emerson and Emerson (V: 512)].

If good language is natural, it is automatically *accessible*, that is, readable, direct, and concise; and Emerson often suggests that this quality of accessibility is readily found in the speech of children. Accessibility requires that a work must be enjoyable to all classes – that is, readable equally in the parlour, the kitchen, and the nursery of every house [Emerson and Emerson (viii: 346)]. For him, the key to readability in English is to balance Germanic with Romance vocabulary: "[O]nly those sentences," he says, "stand, which are good both for the scholar and the cabman, Latin and Saxon; half and half; perfectly Latin and perfectly English" [Emerson and Emerson (viii: 561)]. At any rate, the best writer is one who makes "deep and abstruse things popular" [Emerson and Emerson (ix: 117)]. By that standard, Plato was grand, wrote "from the severity of strength, and is easy to read," whereas his commentators are "grandiose" (often relying upon ornament); and hence, they are difficult to understand [Emerson and Emerson vii: 96)]. Indeed, in Chaucer and the Arthurian lays, the language seems as simple as that of children [Emerson and Emerson (viii: 545)].[47] Similarly, British style from A.D. 1600 - 1700 seems a kind of "baby talk" – again, the force of words one notes in the speech of children [Emerson and Emerson (ix: 438)].

Emerson also appeared to associate accessibility with directness. Thus, though regarding Wordsworth's "Prelude" as a "poetical pamphlet" lacking "texture" [Emerson and Emerson (ix: 151 - 52)], Emerson calls Wordsworth's style "manly" because the poet reports only real thoughts and emotions, concerning himself with the "just value of the dignity of thought," rendered "into simple and sometimes happiest poetic speech" [Emerson and Emerson (x: 267 - 68)]. Speaking in the same vein, Emerson observed that in style, Thoreau "has muscle," born of vivid imagery, as opposed to Emerson's own "sleepy generality"[Emerson and Emerson (ix: 522)], a self-criticism by which Emerson indicts others. To Emerson, the above fault of vagueness or lack of directness seems to plague the poetry of William Ellery Channing, which is unclear in statement, making an impression that is indefinite and hazy, as though it were merely miscellaneous music [Emerson and Emerson (ix: 180)]. Similarly, Collins'[48] "Ode to Evening" "pleases only as music; though, like the strains of an Aeolian Harp," it may restore the lost sights and sounds of a summer evening," becoming, in effect, good whistling [Emerson and Emerson (x: 201)], because it does not make a clear enough statement. In the same way, Tennyson[49] (though brave, inventive, "never harsh or

---

[47] Chaucer, Geoffrey (1343 - 1400). British Medieval Poet and Author of *The Canterbury Tales*. -- Arthurian lays. Series of Medieval poems based upon the apparently fictional King Arthur.

[48] Collins, William (1721 - 1759). British poet and transitional figure between the Augustan and Romantic styles.

[49] Tennyson or Alfred, Lord Tennyson (1809 - 1892). Regarded as the most famous of the British Victorian poets.

obscure," thoughtful, and in some ways humble, with facility, variety, and power in creating rhythmic speech) [Emerson and Emerson (x: 240-41)], lacks "manly compass" because he concerns himself more with the rendering of thought than with the solidity of the thought itself [Emerson and Emerson (x: 267 - 68)]. Thus, rather than merely suggest or insinuate a thought, good rhetoric flies forward to state it directly [Emerson and Emerson (ix: 311-12)].

In addition to readability and directness as aspects of accessibility, Emerson requires the kind of concise language which, again, he finds in the speech of children. He sees concise language as concrete, frank, and overtly descriptive [Emerson and Emerson (v: 435)]; and these descriptions would be such as no dictionaries, but events and character only could illustrate" [Emerson and Emerson (v: 249)]. This language is naturally economical, omitting "the unnecessary word" and saying "the greatest things in the simplest way" [Emerson and Emerson (viii: 449)].[50] Emerson's admiration for this type of economical approach is evidenced in his approval of the opinions of Samuel Rowse, a crayon portraitist of the day, when Rowse proclaims that a portrait should be made by a few continuous strokes, giving the great lines; but if made by labour and by many corrections, though it became at last accurate, it would give an artist no pleasure, would look muddy" [Emerson and Emerson (ix: 154)].[51] Presumably, then, if the writer speaks a fact plainly, directly, and economically, the reader will find it fully accessible and would discover it impossible to omit any of what was spoken because the writer already has omitted every superfluous word

---

[50] One has to wonder whether Emerson is expressing early some of the tenets of Imagism.
[51] The journal's Footnote 2 refers to the American illustrator and lithographer Samuel Worcester Rowse (1822 – 1901), who completed portraits of both Emerson and Henry David Thoreau.

[Emerson and Emerson (ix: 436-437)]. Perhaps for this reason alone, Emerson would agree with Edgar Allan Poe[52] that poems do not need to be long; for when they are, according to Emerson, they are "[b]orrowers of eternity" [Emerson and Emerson (v: 441)].

In addition to naturalness and accessibility, language must be *magnetic*, must carry special emotive power, so as, again, to hold the attention of the reader. This power is most easily conferred by control, which places the writer in constant charge of all of the language effects; exuberance, which ensures that one of the effects is emotional intensity; and color, which is responsible for surface attraction.

According to Emerson audiences are attracted to work that demonstrates an executive power or control in the use of language. Ostensibly, this executive power places writers in complete command of everything they say, including their expression of associated qualities of exuberance and color. As a result, their language is neither "imitative" nor "purely ornamental," since this type of writer has recognized that "everything of beauty for beauty's sake is embellishment, non-functional embellishment: that is false, childish and moribund" [Emerson and Emerson (vi: 208-09; viii: 320; ix, 460)].

This executive ability is often demonstrated by the ease, flexibility, and colloquial or idiomatic quality of the phrasing. No one possessed so much of this executive power as Dante, a master of rhetoric, even though he often used homely subjects as the basis of his poetry [Emerson and Emerson (viii: 33)].[53] For Emerson,

---

[52] Poe, Edgar Allan (1809 - 1849). Influential American Romantic poet and critic, best known for his gothic poems and short stories.

[53] Dante or Durante di Alighiero degli Alighieri (1265 - 1321). Premier Italian poet, political theorist, and author of *The Divine Comedy*.

this power is characteristically expressed in the 16th Century by ease and flexibility, accompanied by a remarkable prodigality and intellectual abundance [Emerson and Emerson (viii: 287)]. Shakespeare's style, though consisting of observations reflecting "the widest knowledge of men," conveyed ease of phrase [Emerson and Emerson (viii: 367)], and "Shakespeare's speeches in *Lear* are in the very dialect of 1843" [Emerson and Emerson (vi: 400)]. An example contemporary to Emerson, is Thomas Carlyle,[54] who especially demonstrates "force of statement" and "executive power in the use of English" [Emerson and Emerson (ix: 529)], in that his style suggests the spontaneity and the vitality of conversation [Emerson and Emerson (ix: 361)], and his type of "projectile" style echoes in all good writing [Emerson and Emerson viii: 261 – 62, 561)].[55]

The exuberance, joy, and utter absorption in the work exhibited by the artist contributes to magnetic power. This means that poetry, like all other art, must delight the author first; and the same joy experienced by the writer will likewise affect the reader [Emerson and Emerson (x: 301)]. Thus, the "masters painted and carved for joy, and knew not that virtue had gone out of them" [Emerson and Emerson (viii: 499)]. For this reason, perhaps, Emerson praises the "abandon" in Michelangelo which he finds somewhat lacking in Milton [Emerson and Emerson (v: 307; viii: 164)]. Through hyperbole, Emerson expresses this notion of exuberance when he observes that readers are likewise affected when authors write with their whole self and spirit. Shakespeare seems to have written his works by hurling his body "at the mark when [his] arrows [were]

---

[54] Carlyle, Thomas (1795 - 1881). British Victorian essayist, philosopher, and historian.

[55] Though Emerson seems annoyed by the fact that, to him, Carlyle never "much uncover[s] his secret mind," he does feel that Carlyle has contributed to writing by expanding its rhetorical range: "He writes with remarkable flexibility and expression, suggestive of the timely fluctuations of the wind -- high, low, loud, emphatic, understated, jocular, querulous -- in fact, a living narrative." Emerson was speaking specifically of Carlyle's *Life of John Sterling*.

spent, like Cupid in Anacreon" [Emerson and Emerson (vi: 400)].[56] In like manner, "The old writers, such as Montaigne, Milton, Browne, when they had put down their thoughts, jumped into their books bodily themselves, so that we have all that is left of them in our shelves; there is not a pinch of dust beside" [Emerson and Emerson (viii: 502)].[57]

Tone is a necessary complement of this joy. Tone must be considered an aspect of exuberance because the wrong tone can sap the piece, when what is actually needed is greatness of thought, which expresses "a finer moral sentiment," thereby drawing forth eloquence. This is because "eloquence is a war of posts. What is said is the least part of the oration. It is the attitude taken, the unmistakable sign never so casually given (in the tone of voice, or manner, or word), that a greater spirit speaks from you than is spoken to in him" [Emerson and Emerson (ix: 435; viii: 242)]. The charm and potency of eloquence is that the writer "threaten[s] in every sentence to say somewhat new, bright, fatal .... Here is mere play, play of genius, improvisation for the artist's own delight, and out of the midst of it he hurls a winged word that becomes a proverb of the world and conquers kings, and clothes nations in its colors" [Emerson and Emerson (viii: 221)]. Such writing will "not be fossilized or evoke death." But rather writing should consist of "spermatic, prophesying, man-making words" [Emerson and Emerson (vi: 132-33)]. In point of fact, an arid or angry tone will always be inferior to an ironic, deeply human one like

---

[56] Cupid. Son of Venus and either Mars or Mercury and god of all the varieties of love; he is usually thought of as capricious or arbitrary in choosing the victims of his arrows. -- Anacreon (c. 583 BC – 485 BC). Greek lyric poet.

[57] The inclusion of Milton here is paradoxical, given Emerson's slightly dismissive comment about Milton's lack of "abandon," above. -- Montaigne (1533 - 1594). Michel Eyquem de Montaigne. French philosopher and master of the essay as a literary and philosophical form. -- Browne, William (1590-1645). British pastoral poet.

that adopted by Socrates [Emerson and Emerson (ix: 520)]. The angry, railing tone of the contemporary group of liberal reformers was to Emerson a case in point. Their vice was that, behind so much shouting, they offered no new ideas, leaving the young, hopeful idealists "turning away with a kind of bitterness from the saturation of talk, of promise, and of preaching. Silence, personal prowess, cheerfulness, solid doing, seem to be the natural cures" [Emerson and Emerson (v: 528-29)]. In fact, "if your word threatens me, I know it is a bully, I know it is weak, I know there is a better word discoverable and returnable" [Emerson and Emerson (v: 537-38)]. Indeed, Emerson admits, "I often think how hard it is to say with sweetness [your] thought, when you know that it affronts and exasperates your audience. It is even [more] difficult to write it for such readers without leaving on the line some bitterness" [Emerson and Emerson (x: 265)]. The remedy for the writer is to "[o]mit all the negative propositions" and "electrify us by perpetual affirmations, unexplained" [Emerson and Emerson (ix: 85)]. That word only which is fair and fragrant, which blooms and rejoices, which runs before me like verdure and a flowering vine, sowing an Eden in the path, is truth" [Emerson and Emerson (v: 537-38)], and the expression of such truth is ever exuberant and full of joy.

Possibly a third aspect of magnetic appeal is color, and the routine, scientific definition of color as "the quality of an object or substance with respect to light reflected by the object" is perhaps revealing for us, here. For color is also a way of grabbing the attention of readers by offering to them a surface which is magnetic expressly because it is prismatic. Emerson asserts that this quality of color is often acquired by diversity of social connections [Emerson and Emerson (viii: 178)]: "Nothing so marks a man as bold imaginative expressions." Such writing, distinguishable from mere drill, always exhibits" the audacities of genius" [Emerson and Emerson (vii: 198)]; yet this kind of eloquence is by no means automatic [Emerson and Emerson (vii: 245)]. For "If [writers surpass] everybody in mother wit, yet [are] scholar like the rest, be sure [they have] got a mother or father or aunt or cousin who has the uncorrupted slang of the street, the pure mud, and which is inestimable to [them] as spice and alterative [sic], and which delights you in [their] rhetoric, like the devil's tunes when put to slow time in church music" [Emerson and Emerson (ix: 436)].[58] Emerson extends his principle of stylistic color even to orators – perhaps, especially to orators – comparing them to poets, both of whom "must be cunning Daedaluses and yet made of milk like the mob": The orator "must have a dash of the devil in him," and "his rhetoric must be satanic" [Emerson and Emerson (vii: 205)].[59] Emerson believes that such color was prominent in Elizabethan drama: "The old dramatists wrote the better for the great quantity of their writing and knew not when they wrote well. The playhouse was low enough to have entire interest for them; they were proprietors; it was low and popular and their comrades evidently thought the mass of old plays or of stage plays *corpus vile*, in which any experiment might be freely tried. Had the prestige which hedges about a modern tragedy or other worthless literary work existed, nothing could have been done. The coarse but warm blood of the living English circulated in the plays as in street ballads ...." [Emerson and Emerson (vii: 88-9)]

Thus, however elusive may be this question of development, the above reveals the primary issues about which Emerson shows the most concern. It is obvious that he abhors and is far from interested in constructing a book of rules. In fact, for Emerson

---

[58] This service was rendered to Emerson by his aunt, Mary Moody Emerson (1774 – 1863).
[59] Emerson means, mischievous, playful, boisterous, or jocular.

the Transcendentalist, this type of thinking would be impossible. But he has spent much time brooding over the stylistic possibilities, and we must be careful to acknowledge them.

c. <u>Refining the Designed and Fleshed-Out Vehicle</u>. In addition to the processes of design and development, the resultant literary vehicle must undergo a stage of refinement that raises the level of its artistry and thereby improves its value as a created object. Emerson seems especially interested in this issue because, to him, artistry in his time had declined, judging, he says, from his review of illustrations in modern books [Emerson and Emerson (viii: 280)]. In them, "we see the house that is building and not the house that is built [Emerson and Emerson (vi: 97 - 98)]. Similarly, modern musical artists appeared "Partial, like mutilated eunuchs...."[Emerson and Emerson (ix: 449)] Emerson seems to say something similar of contemporary writers when he laments that neither in England nor America does he find an overabundance of skillful authors [Emerson and Emerson (vii: 29)]. Apparently, the refinement which Emerson sought involves perspective, proportion, and selectivity, qualities which might be illustrated by analogy to architecture. In this analogy, Emerson apparently would view perspective as the clear goal which the builder must keep in mind during the entire process of building. It is the most important skill which a writer can possess, at this stage. Proportion may represent the general plan of construction drawn by reason, which makes possible the relationship between part and part and part and whole. It is consequently synonymous with the building impulse itself. Selectivity connotes the polish and outward beauty of the completed building. This architectural analogy is, of course, ludicrous because imperfect; at the same time, it is useful, in that it helps us to pin down the abstractions with which Emerson seems to have been struggling.

Perspective allows the writer to arrive at the core or hidden meaning behind the work, which ultimately is the most important accomplishment. The aim of writers is to "uncover beauty; that is verily [their] work; in that block of stone, in that rough verse, to free the noble conception, until it shall be as truly God's work as is the globe of the earth, or the cup of the lily" [Emerson and Emerson (vii: 216)]. This sentiment, we know, was voiced by Emerson earlier, when he asserted that, though the writer will always be frustrated with the finished product, his aim should be, not only to imitate Nature as closely as possible, but even more, to create something new in Nature; to give birth, in effect, to another "creature" in Nature. Indeed, as we will see later, part of Emerson's theory of the social impact of any work rests upon the expectation that the work exhibit great beauty, because it is through this beauty that readers may first become motivated to reach or long for something higher than themselves. Without the writer's perspective, the desired refinement (and, thereby, completion) of the finished vehicle is all but impossible. Not only would writers then not perceive clearly enough the goal which they want to achieve and hence the outlines of their object would remain hazy, but also they would have no standard by which to render final artistic placement of the details of their object, with the result that they are never in the position to evoke real beauty, which, to Emerson, presupposes clarity of form and elegance of detail.

Having mastered perspective, artists learn to render their plan or it may be their carefully constructed thoughts with a keen

106

sense of *proportion*, because proportion adds to the production of "permanence, beauty, grandeur" [Emerson and Emerson (v: 36)]. To accomplish this admittedly ambitious aim, writers need distance from their creative object, achieved not only by something as exalted as their genius [Emerson and Emerson (vi: 514)], but also simply by time spent away from the piece [Emerson and Emerson (viii: 35)].[60] Indeed, when the final judgment is rendered, the writer will find that the "material is nothing; proportion is all" [Emerson and Emerson (vi: 296)]. We have to believe that artists instinctively appreciate the necessity for proportion because they find it in Nature in the forms of rhythm, periodicity, and alternation [Emerson and Emerson (viii: 241)]. They see this rhythm in Nature in surprising resemblances, patterns, or repetitions, such as are observed when we note, and derive pleasure from, "the figure of the oak leaf on the under shell of the tortoise...." [Emerson and Emerson (x: 219-20)] Borrowing from Nature, the writer also embodies this repetition in rhetoric and in the rhyme and rhythm of poetry; the priest, in the liturgical utterances of the church; the engineer and craftsman, in optics and acoustics; and the architect, in structural regularity. Emerson might also have added the subtle sequencing of chords found in music. And this periodicity is likewise expressed in tone and rhythm" [Emerson and Emerson (x: 298)]. In utterances, "[N]o number of echoes," and in architecture no number of "colonnades," displease [Emerson and Emerson (ix: 447)]. "The same periodicity ... reigns in fable, and brings the wildest curve round to a true moral, [just] as [do natural displays] in electricity, gravitation, and the crystal. In poetry specifically, the melody is everything, more important

---

60 These perceptions, of course, echo Horace's daunting advice to writers in *Ars Poetica* ("Epistle to the Pisos"), and re-asserted by Alexander Pope in "Epistle to Dr. Arbuthnot," that they should keep their work unpublished for at least nine years.

than the thought or meaning [Emerson and Emerson (ix: 311)], an opinion which Emerson, again, had uttered earlier – that it is "music" and/or "affection" which accounts for ninety-nine percent of successful composition: "I amuse myself often, as I walk, with humming the rhythm of the decasyllabic quatrain, ... or other rhythms, ... I find a wonderful charm, heroic, and especially deeply pathetic or plaintive in cadences, and say to myself, Ah, happy! if one could fill these small measures with words approaching to the power of these beats!" [Emerson and Emerson (viii: 444 - 45)] I learned that the rhyme is there in the theme, thought, and image, themselves" [Emerson and Emerson (ix: 209)], which is why the Pentelican Marble, secure and obedient under the chisel, made the sculptor and why the sea "makes the sailor" [Emerson and Emerson (ix: 487)].

Besides perspective and proportion, refinement or artistry presupposes a special type of *selectivity*. In fact, one of Emerson's core principles seems to be that all writing should be selection in order to drop every dead word, a principle which Emerson somewhat voiced earlier when he spoke of economy of style. "Why do you not save out of your speech or thinking only the vital things, the spirited mot which amused or warmed you when you spoke it, because of its luck and newness?....If [we] would learn to read [our] own manuscript severely, becoming really a third person, and search only for what interested [us, we] would blot to purpose, and how every page would gain! Then all the words will be sprightly, and every sentence a surprise" [Emerson and Emerson (x: 302-03)]. Thus, before writers can expect others to be their patrons, they must first be their own: "What do you bring us slipshod verses for? No occasional delicacy of expression or music of rhythm can atone for stupidities. Here are lame verses, false rhymes, absurd images, which you indulge yourself in; which is as if a handsome person should come into a company with foul hands or face. Read Collins. Collins would have cut his hand off before he would have left, from a weak self-esteem, a shabby line in his ode" [Emerson and Emerson (vii: 183)]. As he has done before, Emerson uses as an example of the lack of selectivity the poetry of William Ellery Channing, which, though displaying the merit of being genuine, and not the metrical commonplaces of the magazine, reveals that he has not kept faith with the reader; 'tis shamefully indolent and slovenly. He should have lain awake all night to find the true rhyme for a verse, and he has availed himself of the first one that came; so that it is all a babyish incompleteness" [Emerson and Emerson (viii: 540-41)]. Real skill endows writers with the power of selection, which "sips the foam of the cup," showing "infinite degrees of delicacy" which "can chip off a scale, where a coarser hand and eye find only solid wall" [Emerson and Emerson (ix: 116)]. With such skill, writers' thoughts penetrate to the fabric of their book; but in the end, without this skill, their thoughts get effaced [Emerson and Emerson (x: 342-43)].

Thus, while perspective allows writers to arrive at the core or hidden significance of their work, while the beauty created by proportion helps to render the literary vehicle permanent (or able to be re-read many times without loss), selectivity seems to endow the finished product with surface clarity and polish.

As we consider the question of literary form as a whole, we find that there are a number of steep challenges for the would-be writer. It is not enough for the writer to be a conduit of the Oversoul: the writer must also possess the power of construction, the ability to convert the inexpressible into the expressible, to master one of the true mysteries of Nature, which is how to give birth to an idea, how to bring it into existence for human benefit. And Emerson has already admitted that the ambitions of many potential writers are aborted because the ability to perceive is not the same as the ability to construct. To construct, writers must first be able to keep a goal in mind and to be disciplined by this goal, even while accepting the fact that they can never achieve the perfection apparent in Nature. Instead, they rely upon the sleight of hand which allows them to build on a parallel (that is, mental and imaginative) plane, in which they can promote the illusion that they are artistic masters who can first visualize and then concretize a literary work worthy – through its conscious design, development, and refinement – of being published.

The main question being posed in the last stage, the Post-Creative Phase, is, what impact does the work have upon the public which receives it? Though Emerson is concerned with the personality conditions which enhance the writer's chances, with how literary subject matter emerges, and with the methods writers employ to give form to their work, he ultimately is interested in didactics – that is, in the ethical and/or instructional or inspirational influence of a piece. Thus, this third or post-creative stage of the life of literature concerns the public's connection to or reception of a given work. As stated above, this latter phase, following, as it does, upon the creative effort of the writer, inaugurates a period in the life of the work somewhat detached from the writer. The initial manifestation of this connection is the cultural appropriation (or publication) of the work, during which stage, writers send their completed work out to a public, relinquishing exclusive control of their creative product. The work then becomes an explicit public property, in that the public, not the writer, shapes the remaining life of the piece. Consequently, the fact that a literary work can make an impression on the reader -- can condition a reader's consciousness – becomes the foundation on which the future of a literary piece must be based, once that piece leaves the control of the writer.

But in this phenomenon of impression, what is truly interesting is the fact that the audience also has something to contribute to the writer, which is its interpretation of the work; its judgment about what the writer has produced; its ability through these judgments to contribute to the literary canon that has resulted from long periods of comparable audience response; and the possibility that in this canon new and even established writers may find information to advance their art which would not ordinarily be available and which might influence them if they create fresh pieces.[61]

The initial manifestation of this third period of the literary creative process is the immediate appropriation of the work, during which stage writers (who can do so) send their completed work out to a public. The work then becomes an explicit cultural or group property, in that the public, and not the writer, shapes the remaining life of this work. It is obvious that the act of publication leads inexorably to the process of cultural reception and then either of cultural preservation or cultural disposal of a work, forcing us to examine what appear to be productive relationships between two seemingly unrelated spheres -- that of writers as the work has emerged in stages from their mind and that of the public as readers have received and culturally absorbed that work. These incongruities turn out to be two seemingly equal halves of a creative whole. If we think in terms of a different metaphor, the work itself is the obvious middle link, relating the writer on the one hand to the audience on the other. We are interested in the way in which these spheres inter-relate to allow the cultural appropriation or non-appropriation of a literary work and the influences flowing from this process. To the extent that the public response is negative, the work drops below the threshold of the public consciousness and disappears,

---

[61] This concern regarding "influence" links Emerson's thinking to the rhetorical theory of writing as articulated by Aristotle and Horace.

as does invariably the writer. The public appropriates the work or rejects it. Hence, the term "cultural appropriation of literature" refers, not only to simple publication, but also to the acceptance or non-acceptance of a work by the public that comes to read or otherwise experience a literary piece; and ultimately, to the process of preservation or of disposal which seems to characterize the history of literature, if not the whole history of art.

If we dig more deeply into this process of appropriation, we note that, during the cultural disposition of a literary product, we witness three events: not just the aforementioned *exposure*, or the writer's release of the product to the public and the public's decisive preservation or rejection of this product; but also *response*, or the mainly psychological influence of this work on the public; and *use*, or the public's move from psychological influence to mental assessment of any work which it does receive and the practical employment of this assessment for the possible benefit of both culture and writer.

In the cultural appropriation of literature, the role of writers themselves is indirect though foundational. It is indirect because, it is the public which now takes center stage, while the author fades into the background; it is foundational because writers must provide the stimulus[62] to which the public responds. This shift of control from the writer to the public is made possible because of three self-evident facts: the writer's investment in the work, the bridging capacity of that work, and the interplay between this work and the public.

1. <u>Investment in the Work</u>. Throughout the previous period of creativity or the construction of the literary vehicle, the writer focused upon one concern -- that of transforming a work from a mental or intuitive impression into a fully-realized or fully-materialized object. At that time, the writer's primary (perhaps only) concern should have been the excellence of the work for its own sake, and not as a paid thesis [Emerson and Gilman (15: 125 – 126)] or as a way of pursuing a flashy commercial success [Emerson and Gilman (14: 68)]. In this creative period, Henry James[63] has asserted, all we should see of writers "is the back [they turn] to us as [they bend] over [their] work" [James (xxi); Jackson, "Theory")].

---

[62] Stimulus-response is but one of the possible metaphors.
[63] James, Henry (1843 – 1916). Considered one of the greatest American novelists, he sought to make the novel a fine art.

2. **Bridging Capacity**. But we must recognize that there is a clear link between this foundational contribution of the writer and the subsequent direction of the appropriation process, because the power to hold the attention of a potential audience resides in what the writer has previously done with the work's content -- intellectual, emotional, and aesthetic. The expert writer will have relied upon the veracity of the page and its closeness to Nature, experience, or "life" [Emerson and Gilman (13: 425)], rather than upon other books [Emerson and Gilman (14: 364)], the imitation of others, or ways of distorting the vision [Emerson and Gilman (13: 425)]. Guided by "the irresistible beauty or force of the story" [Emerson and Gilman (15: 125 – 126; 16: 341)], writers will have written exclusively "from the love of imparting certain thoughts ...." [Emerson and Gilman (10: 315)] They know intuitively that readers will take up such work only when they discover in it real experiences which they can relate to their own. Thus, if writers have copied, not from their unmoored "fancy," but from fact [Emerson and Gilman (16: 265)], their work will be magnetic and not in danger of being overshadowed" or "supplanted," in the same way that the uniqueness of the oak keeps it from being eclipsed by the palm [Emerson and Gilman (13: 425)]. Given the fact that writers themselves must provide the vital link among themselves, the work, and the appropriating public, these writers, ironically, play an initiating role in the post-creative or cultural appropriation phase of the literary creative cycle. They construct an object which contains the seed of a future relationship with the public. Through their industry, they have built into their work the red thread of Ariadne by which, later, the public either will accept or reject the writer's particular creative product. If a work lacks this internal magnetism, Emerson feels, then authors must blame

themselves if the public turns away, not deeming this work authentic [Emerson and Gilman (16: 114)].

Hence, when they release their work to the public, writers should not have to wonder who will read it; for if they have done their job, the work rises out of the range of writers' concern or responsibility. Writers do nothing further with it and ought to do nothing further, except rest, or renew the creative cycle by attempting other creative projects. They allow their work to speak for itself, even when, from primarily commercial considerations, they are sent out by their publishers to promote what they have produced. It is true, as we will point out later, that writers can enrich this renewal or resetting of the creative cycle by drawing upon the result of the ensuing appropriation process (that is, by learning from the reactions of the public); but until this process is completed, the writer's role as creator of a particular piece is done. By virtue of the magnetic quality built into a work, the public will appropriate it or not, thereby disposing of it as a cultural object; and (if the work is rejected by the public), the unavoidable disposing of writers themselves as cultural voices. But when accepted by the public, the work will acquire a cultural life of its own -- vibrant to the extent that an audience responds to it; or inert, to the degree that the public finds it uninviting.

3. **The Work and the Public**. Having touched upon the role of writers in producing a work which they release to a public, and in which can be found the basis of the public's response, we can examine more closely the interaction between this released work and the public which receives it. To this new creation, the public evidences: an initial interest or disinterest; followed by an

actual choice, in which they either accept or reject a piece, on the basis of its continuing attractive or magnetic appeal; and a final selection phase in which literary pieces become relatively permanent features of the public consciousness, preserved because they prove themselves culturally useful. Thus, the process is threefold: attraction, reexamination, and preservation.

a. <u>Attraction</u>. The initial process by which readers evidence interest or disinterest in a book (and, we have to think, interest in any creative product such as music, painting, film, or sculpture) involves a curious reciprocity between reader and book. On the one hand, the public seems constantly to be searching for the "right" book. And their unique predilections suggest the types of books for which they search. These readers are innately thirsty for works which stimulate them by presenting them with "the overdose of that quality whereof they have the underdose" [Emerson and Gilman (15: 399)] – a quality which presumably writers have contacted from the Oversoul and which it has been their one mission to communicate to the reader. To find such books, readers make "a broad hard-beaten road" to an author's door, "though it be in the woods" [Emerson and Gilman (13: 403)]. Conversely, the content of a book presupposes a certain type of reader. For if a book conveys something valuable to a particular public [Emerson and Gilman (10: 374 – 5; 15: 355)], this book naturally attracts this public -- though, to Emerson (as we have seen in the discussion of style or "voice"), a book achieves its highest when it wins the attention, not only of the scholar, the intellectual, the mystic, or the connoisseur, but also of the modest or unpretentious reader [Emerson and Gilman (10: 51)].

This tendency of an audience to be drawn to a particular book and this capacity of a book to attract its peculiar audience can persist even beyond generations. For, speaking over the heads of a contemporary, but un-responsive, public to the advancing assembly beyond [Emerson and Gilman (15: 176)], a good book can wait centuries for sympathetic readers -- because "there is no age" to good writing, which, "however expressed, saith to us, 'Come out of time, come to me in the Eternal'" [Emerson and Gilman (7: 269)]. Such books remain "unexpensive and harmless" in libraries [Emerson and Gilman (16 130)] until sympathetic readers discover them [Emerson and Gilman (15: 355)]. Thus, if an appropriate audience does not respond when the book first is published, the author can write intimately to some "unknown friend" [Emerson and Gilman (10: 315)], doing so proudly and without explanation [Emerson and Gilman (7: 365)] -- believing, all the while, that the right audience eventually will appear.

b. <u>Reexamination</u>. But it is equally true that a book (to survive beyond the public's initial admiration of it, and hence to attain a more permanent place within a culture) has to induce an audience to return to it, after readers have "[outlived] the dismay or overpowering" of their first impression [Emerson and Gilman (16: 105)]; after, that is to say, the initial impression of the book has worn off. The book's inability to survive during this second part of the selection process indicates, in Emerson's view, the deep literary fault that the piece fails to convey "real experience." Initial admirers "never take it up again, because it makes no impression on their memory; whilst they do remember and return to the page of real experiences...." [Emerson and Gilman (15: 461)] It is this process of selection to which Emerson is referring when he describes what happens when the public encounters the expressions of genius as opposed to the productions of talent: "The books of men of genius are divers or dippers. When they alight on the water, they soon disappear, but after some space they emerge again. Other books are land-birds which, falling in the water, know well that their own safety is in keeping at the top; they flutter and chirp and scream, but if they once get their heads under, they are drowned forever" [Emerson and Gilman (7: 361)]. Given the time the public needs to embrace these skillful "sea birds" and to cull out the shallow "land birds," publishers should produce and then stand by the best literature in the land - - despite the early "placability" of readers, who eventually "will find out when they have a master." In this way, money-capital reveals its real cultural value -- when wealth enables the publisher to hold out for months against negative public opinion until "the discerning minority" of readers, Emerson says, have recognized true merit.

c. <u>Preservation</u>. We find regarding the third stage of selection that once readers have chosen a work [Emerson and Gilman (14: 167)], they often preserve it. In fact, the peculiar sympathy which they have for a book produces a kind of audience allegiance and even solidarity, in that reading the same book links readers, not only to the writer, but also to one another [Emerson and Gilman (15: 425)]. They may even regard an attack upon a book or its author as an assault upon themselves [Emerson and Gilman (8: 49)]. This phenomenon of preservation allows those who can write a good poem of a dozen lines to "rest on their oars forever, ... dear and necessary to the human race and worth all of the old trumpery Plutarchs and Platos and Bacons of the World" [Emerson and Gilman (11: 37)].[64] Writers send "a copy of [their] verse to the printer"; the audience takes charge of it; and the piece not only "flies from

---

[64] Plutarch (46AD – 117AD?). Greek Platonic philosopher, essayist, and historical biographer.

land to land" and "language to language," but also old readers and constant supplies of new readers cherish it. Presumably, too, these readers pass their appreciation of a piece to succeeding generations; and the verse, therefore, continues, slowly expanding its new "life" [Eliot (46)]. This expanded life, as we shall see, may cause the work to become part of the literary canon.

Taken as a whole, then, the cultural appropriation or rejection of a piece depends upon the preferences of the public -- however indeterminate these predilections may be. It is obvious that this initially curious dependency expands the life of a literary piece far beyond its creation; and this very extension is the foundation for the post-creative phase in "the life of literature" which we will further explore when considering just how the work influences its readers -- and the public's reciprocal contribution to the cultural life of the work.

The book undergoes its first test when readers find in the book a quality or message or inspiration which they need and which presumably has come to them from the Oversoul through the agency of the writer. If the audience which values the stimulation embodied in a book does not yet exist, then the book must wait for a future audience. Subsequent to this initial attraction, the book undergoes a second test, which is whether an audience returns to it at a later time, because if it does not, Emerson believes that the book evidences the fatal flaw of not being based upon real experience. However, if this audience attraction continues, the book enters a third and most consequential phase, which is that of preservation, as the public jealously passes the book on from reader to reader and generation to generation. This preservation once again sets the stage for the extension of the public life of the work.

It seems apt that the whole question of the literary creative process should arrive at the idea of the impact of the work upon a public. For unavoidably, writers have placed in their work certain magnetic and reader-attracting threads. Seemingly, these threads provide the stimulations which readers seek -- and which Emerson has described as providing "the overdose of that quality whereof they have the underdose" [Emerson and Gilman (15: 399)]. Presumably, if we are reading Emerson correctly, the beauty and substance which Emerson insists must be aspects of a work, can alter or transform the reader's aesthetic enjoyment, the content of the reader's mind, and, it may be, the reader's spiritual identity. Some readers, it is true, may be attracted primarily by the surface quality of the work – that is, its artistry or beauty. Other readers may be drawn to its intellectual content; and still others, to some perceived ethical or even spiritual quality. Some may find that they are drawn by a combination of the above traits. Thus, Emerson's somewhat exulted theory of the impact of literature is based upon the supposed ability of literature to do one or all of the following: elevate the reader, through the beauty or artistry perceived; effect substantive changes in the thought processes of readers; and alter the identity of the reader, thereby aiding the work of the prophet or seer.

As stated above, the fact that a literary piece can condition a reader's consciousness becomes the foundation on which the future of a literary piece is invariably based, once that piece leaves the control of the writer and is published. Thus, a second (and for Emerson the most critical) expression of this post-creative phase is based upon the way in which the work affects the public, the way in which it adjusts their preconceptions, or the way in which it modifies their spiritual identity or values.

1. **Aesthetic Attraction to the Object**. For Emerson, artistry should render the resulting object so compelling that it can easily attract the audience or consumer; this audience itself must rely upon reason to respond to this first potential catalyst of audience attraction, beauty; and art can then exercise its inherent power of drawing out the best of human impulses.

This aesthetic effect is possible because of what the writer has done to the work. If writers have drawn upon Nature, then the beauty of their work will automatically be "aristocratic" or "differencing," difficult of attainment, sublime [Emerson and Emerson (vii: 385)]. An elevating impact upon the audience is thus possible when the object draws subtly upon the "haughty force" behind all that appears in form and that suggests "the cosmical relations of the object," something of "the immeasurable and divine," which echoes or intimates "the spiritual cause," "the genius," the "generic law" [Emerson and Emerson (ix: 279 - 80)]. Beauty's "occult foundation in inward harmony [Emerson and Emerson (vi: 90)] beneath the pleasing surface leaves us ultimately incapable of understanding or defining it, except to acknowledge that the "complete incarnation of spirit" which absolute beauty entails demands "that there shall be no point from which it is absent, and none in which it abides" [Emerson and Emerson (ix: 58)].[65]

The fact that what attracts the reader is often beneath the obvious surface, requiring sensitivity and thought, indicates that

---

[65] Emerson attributes this statement to J[ames] Elliot Cabot (1821 -- 1903), lawyer, philosopher, and Transcendentalist.

art demands much of the beholder, before the beholder can approach, let alone appreciate, a work [Emerson and Emerson (vi: 445-46)]. Though we are "elevated" by beauty" [Emerson and Emerson (ix: 422)], we can never possess or clutch it [Emerson and Emerson (v: 494)] -- though it is accessible to us to the degree to which we exercise Reason, in the Kantian sense: that is, though Beauty itself cannot result from reasoning, or legislation, or the imposition of rules by the writer, only through Reason can we "have property" in this divine quality [Emerson and Emerson (x: 146)].

In short, the object will have a reforming impact because it demands that, to be worthy of it, we improve ourselves by searching beyond it. Indeed, it is this very reformative possibility that forces us to look imperiously for the transcendence which beauty in the object brings, "and if it do not exist in any one, we feel at liberty to insult over that subject, without end" [Emerson and Emerson (viii: 126)]. Still, there is a limitation in being attracted solely by the beauty of the piece. Readers may find joy in literary beauty for its own sake, just as we may admire this quality in a favorite painting or piece of music. In this case, the attraction is purely aesthetic. Emerson describes how beauty may affect us when he concedes that most lovers of beauty are dazzled by the details and that to have seen many beautiful details cloys us and we are better able to keep our rectitude" [Emerson and Emerson (vi: 499)]. At the same time, he notes a limitation, when he states that even the most beautiful and reverential organ music loses its appeal when we hear it too much -- just as such music seems more gorgeous rarely heard. Behind this notion, certainly, is the thought that art enjoyed primarily for its beauty ceases to appeal to us when repetition renders the performance monotonous or too familiar. Art has its purposes, its times and seasons; and we do ourselves harm when we both over- and under-value it [Emerson and Emerson (vii: 66)]. Oddly, what is true for the enjoyer or consumer of art seems likewise true for its producer; for "is it not ridiculous, this what we do in this languid idle trick that we have gradually fallen into of writing and writing without end? After a day of joy, the beating heart is calmed again by the diary. If grace is given me by all angels and I pray, if then I can catch one ejaculation of humility or hope and set it down in syllables, devotion is at an end" [Emerson and Emerson (vi: 94)].

2. <u>Intellectual Content of the Work</u>. Literature embodies a second potential for audience attraction beyond its aesthetic appeal because it can help us examine and, if need be, alter our deeply-cherished beliefs, and by extension, influence our conduct. Literature can bring about these effects through a chain of impacts: literature can stimulate the reader's imagination; it can encourage certain conceptual revisions; and it as a result can help us reform our behavior.

The imagination of readers is stimulated when literature encourages them to be receptive to otherwise overlooked, external or internal stimuli, allowing individuals to explore (vicariously and therefore without fear) the details of life and, in doing so, ennoble them and themselves [Emerson and Emerson (ix: 234)]. Yet, we must keep in mind that the reader is influenced, not only by the specific information the writer conveys, but also by the mood or tone by which this information is presented. At its best, this firing of "the imagination" [Emerson and Emerson (v: 553)] opens the door to the readers' understanding of their own possible limitations. This understanding is achieved by the writer's practicing a type of deceit that nonetheless differs from that practiced by evil, because in the latter, the benefit goes to

126

the evil doer, whereas in the former the benefit is the reader's. This ability to influence the reader's imagination harkens back to our now recognized notion that literature must operate in a mental universe parallel to that of concrete Nature. This type of influence upon the reader presupposes a special "plasticity" and educability of human beings [Emerson and Emerson (vii: 122)]. Through this presumed plasticity, writers endeavor to convey to their readers that which first charmed their own imagination as authors, so that on the reader this charming influence may have a similar effect [Emerson and Emerson (vi: 35)].

Once readers allow themselves to be responsive in this way, Emerson finds that it is the mood or tone of the piece which affects the reader even more than does the content. He is referring to the "tone" or "mood of mind" into which literature can bring us [Emerson and Emerson (v: 314)]. Emerson's theory (by way of Niebuhr)[66] is that, if the author is in perfect repose, he can move the reader deeply. Serenity of tone and of execution may then produce a corresponding serenity in the listener, observer, or reader [Emerson and Emerson (256)]. Ultimately, then, the question Emerson puts to the reader is, "What is the state of mind [the writer] leaves me in? and What does he add?" [Emerson and Emerson (viii: 126 - 27)] Emerson is implying that conceptual rehabilitation is possible because of "the impatience in every man of his limits" [Emerson and Emerson (v: 553)] and his willingness to rely upon external aids to help him overcome these limits. In some sense, this serenity to which the reader may be led echoes the elevation which the reader can experience from the beauty of a piece. Both of these impulses imply the capacity for rehabilitation and are, in fact, catalysts for achieving this state.

---

[66] Niebuhr, or Barthold Georg Niebuhr (1776 - 1831). German-Danish father of modern historiography, Enlightenment thinker, and historian of ancient Roman civilization.

It matters, then, only that a book stimulates, regardless of the direction -- whether we read for aesthetic appeal, for conceptual stimulation, for "antagonism or for confirmation," for contradiction or anger, for edification or inspiration – as even "good indignation brings one all one's powers" [Emerson and Emerson (vi: 99)]. Thus, though Emerson recognizes the limitation of books, which "can't teach mother wit, sagacity, presence of mind, and humanity" [Emerson and Emerson (ix: 252)], he seems to value books specifically for their ability to stimulate – that is, to help us exceed our limitations, allowing us, as Emerson observes from Edmund Burke,[67] to borrow "the aid of an equal understanding," thereby doubling our own; to use "that of a superior," thereby elevating our own to "the stature of that he contemplates" [Emerson and Emerson (viii: 528)]. Perhaps because of his conviction that literature can expand the horizons of people, Emerson can confidently conclude, "When I find in people narrow religion, I find narrow reading" [Emerson and Emerson (x: 269)].

Obviously, books differ in the quality of their content, and only a few of these books provide true wisdom. "Some books," Emerson observes, "leave us free and some books make us free" [Emerson and Emerson (v: 359)], because "some authors are writers of amount; and some, of quality" -- or, as Emerson paraphrases Schelling,[68] "'Some minds speak about things, and some minds speak the things themselves." Emerson thus laments, "how few authors have given me things," beside "style or rhetoric" [Emerson and Emerson (viii: 126)]. Because, for instance, in the work of Carlyle, Byron, and Samuel Johnson, there is more rhetoric or

---

[67] Burke, Edmund (1729 -- 1797). Irish statesman and conservative political philosopher.
[68] Schelling (or von Schelling), Friedrich Wilhelm Joseph (1775 -- 1854). German Idealist philosopher.

suggestion than intellectuality or wisdom [Emerson and Emerson (vii: 285)],[69] these, to Emerson, seem somehow lacking or shallow. In truth, only a few writers contribute to us "guidance and consolation which are still growing and effective...." [Emerson and Emerson (vii: 158)] How few are those who are "opener of doors" for those who follow, rather than making "the universe a blind alley." One "measure of the impurity of insight" is whether or not works create this type of intellectual independence" [Emerson and Emerson (vi: 525; ix: 503-04)], whether or not they "liberate" us, promoting a "sense of freedom and power" [Emerson and Emerson (vi: 218 - 19)]. Thus, for Emerson, the "costliest benefit of books is to set us free from ourselves also" [Emerson and Emerson (ix: 269)].

   3. **Potentially Spiritual Content**. Even beyond its aesthetic and conceptual features, literature attracts a third potential audience when it augments the work of the prophet or seer – when it achieves what Emerson considers the ultimate for literature, which is to evoke from readers a conviction as to their own immortality. This third attracting potential is quite sobering and places into relief Emerson's entire view of the literary effort; for we must acknowledge that literature: is ancillary to the efforts of the truly wise; is at its best when its focus is spiritual or ethical; and is fulfilling an uplifting and stimulative role, more important than its consoling or entertaining functions.

   a. Literature's Limitation. Though he tends to say so many wonderful things about literature, and though, like other arts such

---

[69] Byron. George Gordon Byron, 6th Baron Byron (1788 – 1824). Influential British Romantic Poet. -- Johnson, Samuel (1709 - 1784). An influential neoclassical writer and literary critic, he was one of the earliest sponsors of a Dictionary of the English Language.

as music, literature has the inherent ability both to elevate and reform the reader, Emerson, in the end, asserts that the literary experience is not a primary, but a secondary, one -- totally ancillary to Being Itself. Emerson has constantly considered the act of Being as, in itself, more important than literature itself; and, we must remember, literature operates in a world merely parallel to that in which concrete Nature operates. Thus, literature is not an end but a means, a tool to bring about something else. Emerson points out, for instance, that were we endowed with the wisdom of Shakespeare or were we to bring ourselves to live in the manner of the prophets or holy men, we could dispense with their writings [Emerson and Emerson (v: 258)]. The assumption is that seers, already knowing right conduct, live admirably ethical lives and that, by their example, they are successful in "subduing [all] to order and virtue" [Emerson and Emerson (viii: 353)]. The point is that, in accomplishing their ends, these prophets advert to no books or arts that literature could supply -- only to dread ideas and emotions [Emerson and Emerson (v: 334)].

All that can be said is that, as its main function, literature at most can enhance the work of the wise. This capacity explains why, for Emerson, the moral is ever "the measure of health" in literature [Emerson and Emerson (vii: 248)] and stands at the center of poetry, even eventually, making "poetry" of us all [Emerson and Emerson (vi: 537)]. Stated poorly, the "Muse" helps the wise to "mend the bad world" [Emerson and Emerson (vii: 149)]. Not only literature but also music, even "sculpture and drawing," can induce one to lead a better life [Emerson and Emerson (viii: 556-57)]. However, literature is better-suited to this moral role than other such arts because it has the peculiar power of affecting readers despite their class or position: In that "[m]orals differ from

130

intellectuals in being instantly intelligible to all" [Emerson and Emerson (vii: 250)], literature, at its best when widely accessible, brings "the oracle of conscience," exhibits limitless strength and "domestication," and can make" the poor and uncultivated feel that it addresses them also" [Emerson and Emerson (x: 326-27; v: 488)].

Indeed, as we have been implying, literature can promote "sallies and recoveries of the Soul" and rekindle belief in the inner values [Emerson and Emerson (v: 483 -84)]. We should not forget that the "sacred," the "sweet" function of writers and scholars is "to gather the flowers of the past, to express the essence of old wisdom, to hold the unruly present firm to the sphere, to keep the first cause in mind, and to consecrate all to an aim...." [Emerson and Emerson (viii: 480-81)] Through these avenues, literature awakens in us the very feeling of immortality: The names of Scaliger, Cardan, Galen, Sallust, Livy, suggest ideas of immortal leisure, of elegance and Olympian thoughts.[70] And the reading these books, or the exercise of the same faculties in compositions of our own, makes, for the time, death somewhat incredible and out of nature" [Emerson and Emerson (v: 340)].

b. Literature's Potential. Thus, for Emerson, literature comes into its own when it evidences moral or ethical power but becomes pointless when robbed of this capacity. Doubtless, an illustration of the fact that literature loses its purpose when the ethical sense is not its center, is our detecting "discord and limitation in men of rare talent in whom [the moral] sentiment

---

[70] Scaliger or Joseph Justus Scaliger (1540 - 1609). French scholar of the classical world. -- Cardan. This apparently refers to Italian scientist and philosopher Gerolamo Cardano (1501 - 1576), who wrote among other pieces a treatise, *Immortality of the Soul*. -- Galen of Pergamon (129AD – 210AD). Greek physician, philosopher, and founder of modern medicine. -- Sallust or Gaius Sallustius Crispus (86BC – 35BC). Roman political theorist and historian. -- Livy (59BC – 17AD). Prolific Roman historian.

has not its healthy or normal superiority; as, Byron, Voltaire, Daniel Webster" [Emerson and Emerson (x: 330 - 31)],[71] who, lacking the "key to the moral powers," are apt "to strain all [their] stage tricks of grimace, of bodily terror, of murder, and the most approved performances of Remorse." A book from them which "begins and ends without a poetic ray ... perishes in the reading" [Emerson and Emerson (v: 260)]. For these reasons, Emerson, lamenting that in 1852 no truly moral or spiritual literature existed in Britain or America, asks sadly, Who "gives high counsels to these twin nations? Who points their duties, admonishes, animates, and holds them up to their highest aim? Wordsworth spoke, Milton-like, to their soul. Carlyle by jerks and screams scolded, and sneered. But what high, equal, calm soul held them to their aim?" [Emerson and Emerson (viii: 342)]

In point of fact, we have the notion that literature, in inducing readers to face their illusions about the real world, is capable of accomplishing even more by helping these readers to substitute a liberating wisdom in place of these illusions. The most important illusion which literature causes the reader to confront is the primacy of form. This illusion has heretofore restricted the reader to an animal or infantile state: "The first illusion that is put upon us in the world is the amusing miscellany of colours, forms, and properties. Our education is through surfaces and particulars. Nature masks under ostentatious sub-divisions and manifold particulars the poverty of her elements, and the rigid economy of her rules. And, as infants are occupied wholly with surface-differences, so multitudes of adults remain in the infant or animal state, and never see or know more" [Emerson and Emerson

---

[71] Voltaire (1694 - 1778). Highly influential French Enlightenment philosopher and essayist. -- Webster, Daniel (1782 - 1852). American lawyer and statesman.

(x: 123 - 24)]. Literature provides a method of liberation from this so-called animal condition.

In fact, literature opens a mental gate "into the world" (Emerson would possibly say, "the real or subjective world") whereas, Emerson asserts, mere facts leave us outside [Emerson and Emerson (ix: 88)]. That is why Emerson can come to believe that the "poet is here ... to dwarf and destroy all merely temporary circumstances and to glorify the perpetual circumstance of [humankind]...." [Emerson and Emerson (vi: 410)] Literature, by destroying the primary illusion which matter creates, affords readers a potent method by which to spiritualize themselves and their life. Through the poet's work and that of her or his fellow writers, literature affords us "a platform whence we may command a view of our present life" [Emerson and Emerson (v: 408)], lifting the curtain from the common, ... showing ... that gods are sitting disguised in this seeming game of gypsies and peddlers" [Emerson and Emerson (v: 553)]. For this reason, "students should be educated, not only in the intelligence of, but also in the sympathy with, the thought of great poets" [Emerson and Emerson (x: 31)] and trained "in poverty to a nobler style of manners than any palace can show [them], by Plato and Plutarch, by the Cid, and Sidney, and George Herbert, and Chaucer" [Emerson and Emerson (x: 132)].[72] Shakespeare especially reminds us of the unreality of our everyday living. Because of him, "the world appears so empty. He has educated you with his painted world, and this real one seems a huckster's shop" [Emerson and Emerson (vii: 140)]. This type of education makes the student cheerful and confident in the old

---

[72] Cid. This refers to the epic, *The Song of El Cid*, based upon the Spanish Medieval hero, Rodrigo Díaz de Vivar (? - 1099). -- Sidney, Sir Philip (1554 - 1586). Elizabethan poet, scholar, and courtier. -- Herbert, George (1593 - 1633). One of the main purveyors of the British metaphysical school of poetry.

barbarous routine, whether of politics, or religion, or commerce, or social arrangement. Nature will not longer be kinged, or churched, or colleged, or drawing-roomed as before" [Emerson and Emerson (x: 264)].

Once the illusion of form has been somewhat dissipated, literature takes us a step further by at least suggesting the world that the primacy of form has in the past hidden from us. Literature reveals the true reason that the poet is to be valued: because "all of the arguments and all of the learning is [*sic*] not in the Encyclopaedia or the Treatise on Metaphysics, or the Body of Divinity, but in the sonnet and the tragedy" [Emerson and Emerson (v: 483 - 84)]. Indeed, for Emerson, "the only teller of news is the poet" [Emerson and Emerson (v: 478)].

c. <u>Literature's Other Roles</u>. Obviously, then, for Emerson, the ethical role or utilitarian function of literature will supersede the use of literature for consolation or entertainment. Though Emerson sees a limited value in the use of literature for consolation, he appears to ignore or disdain the use of literature for entertainment and seldom comments on this function. However, on its subsidiary ability to console, Emerson seems to say a bit more, when he asserts that literature resembles music; for just as, when "people are grieved, we go over the sorrow in words, and the more cunning the repetition of it in words, the better consoled they are," and just as "Pythagoras cured distemper with music," so, we "administer" literature -- that is, "we lend them a book" like "*Suspira de Profundis*"[73] or Milton [Emerson and Emerson (vii: 265 - 66)]. Still, there is a limitation even to

---

[73] *Suspira de Profundis*. A work of so-called psychological fantasy, in which the author, Thomas Penson De Quincey (1785 - 1859), develops the genre of addiction literature, as he explores some of the subjective experiences of his opium addiction.

this role of consolation, especially if it is primarily the beauty of a piece that consoles us. This statement is subtlety different from the above idea that certain readers are attracted to a work because of its inherent beauty. In that case, they find joy in beauty for its own sake, but in this case, the attraction is emotional rather than aesthetic. But these two cases do have in common the thought that art ceases to delight or to console when repetition renders the performance monotonous or too familiar. Therefore, Emerson easily reverts to the conclusion that when "[l]iterature is resorted to as consolation" rather than "as decalogue," "then is literature defamed and disguised" [Emerson and Emerson (vii: 15)].

It is on this utilitarian platform (namely, that literature is at its best when it aids the work of the seer) that Emerson's theory of literature ultimately rests. In some senses, this theory has come full circle, in that the struggles of the writer are consummated in the intensified aesthetic and intellectual sensitivity and spiritual awareness of the reader. The channel of communication which the writer has sought to open between the Oversoul and the reader is complete, and this connection between the Oversoul and the reader which the writer has made possible, can never be gainsaid. First, Emerson suggests that a key magnet for the reader is the sheer beauty of a piece, because beauty itself has in it the capacity to elevate. This is the ability to make us yearn to be better than ourselves, to reach for something sublime rather than remain in a state that is frustratingly ugly and pedestrian. A second magnet that attracts the reader is the intellectual content of the work, and in some sense, this is frequently the most common motive for reading. This intellectual avenue offers readers the opportunity of comparing the components of their own mind with those of other minds and, by so doing, proffers the opportunity of revising one's own concepts. The third and ultimate magnet attracting a reader to a piece is the potential ability of literature to aid in the work of the seer, which is to inspire us, to help us discover the soul within us, and to lead a much better spiritual life.

We have been considering the post-creative phase of the life of literature and have found, first, that what the writer has put into the work will determine whether it will survive in the cultural consciousness; and second, that a book which does survive contains threads of beauty, content, or inspiration that attract, and demand allegiance from, the reader. A third (and less obvious) manifestation or iteration of the post-creative phase of the life of literature is a shadowy or less certain phenomenon than either the attraction of the audience to the work after publication or the psychological impact of the work on this audience, in that this third iteration involves what happens after the public has received and been influenced by the work. Thus, this final chapter is added because logic strongly compels it, even though this writer, at least, holds to the notion of the absolute freedom of the author, and he does not wish in this discussion to fall down the rabbit hole of thinking with T.S. Eliot in "Tradition and the Individual Talent"[74] that the writer owes to tradition (by which he means the literary canon) so much as Eliot supposes. What this discussion does wish to explore are certain practical or useful implications that help us exhaust the subject of the literary creative process and the trajectories which the mind of the creative writer might follow. Specifically, the writer has initiated a chain of effects which can bend back upon writers themselves,

---

[74] "Tradition and the Individual Talent." Essay by Thomas Stearns Eliot published in 1919, laying out Eliot's theory of the deep debt which every poet is said to owe to the tradition which preceded his work. Eliot, Thomas Stearns (1888 - 1965). Influential Anglo-American poet and literary critic, best known for the modernist poem *The Waste Land*.

to affect what they may produce in the future. This potential reflex action refers to the impact of the public's reactions upon writers, even though, by this phase of the process, the writer has faded far into the background.

Here, potentially, the audience itself makes an intellectual, not just an emotional, contribution; for, in time, an observer will witness the public's altering its relationship to a published work because of the distance from the piece afforded by time; rendering analytical judgments about this work, however questionable or however valid these judgments may be; and either through a canon or through contemporary feedback, making these judgments available for the use of both new and established writers. It would be helpful to examine these presumably final processes with greater care.

1. <u>From Adoration to Judgment</u>. We have said that the main concern of writers should be that of producing quality work; but we are here suggesting that, once they have done their best to do so, and once they have sent the work out, it undergoes a cycle of selection on its own terms, according to the responses of the public. Thus, we are again speaking both of the responsibility of writers to their work and of the dynamic connections between this completed work and a public which selects it – as something different transpires when a public is not just attracted to a piece and is not just benefiting from it, but is beginning to make intellectual judgments about it. We are speaking, of course, of the activity which we have come to call literary criticism, for lack of a better term. For one of the forces operating in addition to the processes, first of a writer's creation and then of the public's selection and preservation of what has been created, is the audience development occurring after these activities: we are speaking of the undeniable audience process called judgment. Works seem to elicit from the public, not only a degree of acceptance and love, but also a response that is by nature analytical.

We say that judgments about literature are inevitable because, eventually, a change can occur in the way in which readers relate to a work -- a shift from an instinctual or an emotional attachment (such as transpires during selection and preservation), to an intellectual response. Feeling that it has something to give them, readers have sought out the writer's work. Through the "transmission" of sensations, emotions, or ideas, this work bridges the natural distance in consciousness between writer and reader – similar to the existential distance between any two human beings and to the elimination of which, presumably inspired by the Oversoul, earnest writers devote all of their efforts. Then, suddenly, just as, before, writers were "lover[s] loving," embracing their art and tending its growth [Emerson and Gilman (11: 417)], so now the alert reader, by virtue of this "communication," becomes the "lover advised," attempting to appreciate, and ultimately to understand the writer's product. Perhaps ominously, the light thrown upon the work because of this "advisement" becomes a judgment day in which the true separates itself from the false and by means of which the "merriest poem, the sweetest music" ultimately receives from otherwise devoted readers a reluctant, sober, and discriminating critique [Emerson and Gilman (10: 94)]. Thus, as we have stated, during this public reaction to a work, some readers undergo a kind of metamorphosis, from responsive or adoring recipients, to potentially detached observers; from being essentially emotive toward the work, to being fundamentally analytical.

139

2. **The Nature and Validity of Literary Judgment**. In light of this potential shift in the reader's own approach from appreciation to critique, the problem then becomes the very judgments about literature which the reader makes. For, in Emerson's view, these judgments are unsound when they are needlessly destructive, when they fail to take into account the writer's overall genius, and when they are not allowed to mature in time.

Primarily, Emerson is wary of destructive criticism -- by which he means assessments that are aimless, prejudiced, or hyper-analytical. He considers aimless criticism to be "rubbish" [Emerson and Gilman (10: 331)] because the critic writes and speaks merely for the sake of writing and speaking. Though the "borer on our peach trees bores that she may deposit an egg," "the borer[s] into theories and institutions and books [bore] that [they] may bore" [Emerson and Gilman (7: 457)]. Emerson likewise is wary of critics who impose their prejudices or private confusion upon a work; for doing so ruins their credibility. Here, the reader fails to distinguish a "private consciousness from the consciousness that is universal" [Emerson and Gilman (10: 312)]. Just as we have pointed out earlier, in speaking of the detachment that writers must bring to the process of choosing a subject (a process requiring that they distinguish between the universal and the purely private), so here Emerson offers a complementary concept when he emphasizes the obligation of the reader also to learn a degree of detachment and to distinguish the universal from the private. Further, suspicious of overly-analytical readers, Emerson observes caustically that, in the evaluation of literature, "the analytic mind will not carry us far"; that "[t]aking to pieces is the trade of those who cannot construct"; and that the deepest critical insights come to us, not from professors of the academy, but casually from a few astute readers. [Emerson and Emerson (ix: 147)]

Instead of being aimless, prejudiced, or overly analytical, Emerson asserts that criticism should be synthetic. In fact, in a healthy mind, Emerson observes, these critical and synthetic or integrative faculties are naturally complementary and function harmoniously. Such minds, while keenly grasping "differences," overlook surface faults, exhibit the power to generalize, and tend to emphasize the genius of the whole [Emerson and Gilman (14: 197 - 98)], rather than particular faults. Accordingly, knowing that all gifts are fated, not chosen, the best critics encourage authors to learn equally from their successes and failures, their strengths and weaknesses. Realizing that "the world is farmed out to many contractors" and that "each arranges all things on his petty task, sacrifices all for that," these critics will avoid asking writers to produce other than what is natural to their talent; for they see that making such requests is "like advising gunpowder to explode gently, or snow to temper its whiteness, or oak trees to be less profuse in leaves and acorns, or poplars to try the vinous habit and creep on walls" [Emerson and Gilman (10: 149)]. Thus, critics not only should promote the best, the most affirmative" qualities in a writer; but also (Emerson seems slyly to imply) they should support those writers whose very talent is "affirmative," forward-looking, and "vital" [Emerson and Gilman (8: 174)].

The public can accentuate the above critical strengths and diminish the indicated weaknesses by allowing their judgments to mature in time, which confers perspective; makes possible individual assessments, in light of publicly-acknowledged standards; recognizes the impermanence of such standards; and reminds us, in fact, of the ultimate relativity of every human judgment, or achievement.

First, through time, readers are apt to revise their initial judgment of individual works. They more and more may value the seemingly sparse and disagreeable achievements in literature the more they themselves attempt to replicate what they once despised. By this measure, "[a]n intelligent youth," finding "little wonderful" in the work of the ancients, comes through experience to see the excellence of their "confessedly tame and stark poems...." [Emerson and Gilman (8: 280)] Second, the public, in comparing one work to another, gradually recognizes so-called literary models or "masterpieces," against which readers tend to judge the success of other works. And it is here that the literary canon is necessarily born. Third, readers come to entertain the possibility that, in the future, publics may encounter works which dwarf the achievement of even the "masterpieces," such as Shakespeare's, that in the West have become standards of judgment; and that, therefore, such standards themselves may be considered transient effects of the intellectual and spiritual condition of a given age.

Through this third and much more sobering perception, the public begins to accept the absolute relativity, not only of the stature of the actual literary artifacts with which new works are constantly being compared, but also of all judgments of literature. Indeed, the public comes to learn that, not just the greatest instances of literary merit, but indeed any intellectual achievement, reveals only the limitations of an age. For this reason, literature is merely a temporary phase of human activity; and "the entire extant product of the human intellect" is "only one age, revisable, corrigible, reversible" [Emerson and Gilman 7: 352)], by future eras, a concept which echoes the previously-

142

stated notion that, were we to live as the saints live, we could easily dispense with our esteemed literature.

All of these limitations of judgment presuppose humility in making literary assessments, the immediate value of which depends upon the perspective and experience of the age which makes them. In these judgments, time plays a decisive role -- modifying a reader's evaluation of individual works; supplying a canon of public models against which to compare these works; and throwing into relief the impermanence of these very culture-bound standards, by pointing to the unlimited horizons opening up before human creative capacity, in general. These are distant and perhaps overly-fastidious notations which come into play whenever we consider any judgments about a work, but these limitations of the judgments which the public may create (namely, overanalysis, the lack of synthesis, and the failure to allow judgments to mature in time), are nonetheless worth mentioning.

3. **The Potential Value of the Public's Judgment**. If even apparently valid assessments of literature are relative and impermanent, of what use can they possibly be? These judgments, when viewed together over time, constitute a consensus about the features of "successful" writing, if "success" is defined as engaging, and indeed drawing a commitment from, the public, fulfilling the original aim of any work: to reach, to penetrate into the psyche of, and to effect some type of cultural benefit to an audience. Thus, in this final stage of appropriation, which we may alternately call the Social Use of Literary Judgment, we see the formation of what we now think of as "a literary canon" (or somewhat arbitrary yet enduring body of

literary examples and standards which a culture values and seeks to preserve). We say "standards" because the canon consists not only of what are deemed "classics," but these classics are selected (as many of us agree) by a gradually emerging set of implicit "rules," reminiscent of the theological doctrines of the old ecclesiastic canons. Hence, what is implied is a literary theology or orthodoxy. Of course, this perception about the canon is by no means new! However, its orthodoxy is considered by many to be deleterious to literary creativity. But we do have to concede, in all fairness, that the judgments embodied in the canon or those contemporary assessments which are destined to wind up in the canon, may do three useful things: promote the preservation of previously selected works, facilitate the selection of new works, and educate in different ways both the new and the established writer. This last educational effect especially, suggests an important consequence (and some may say, benefit) of audience judgment, as embodied in, or soon to be embodied, in the canon.

a. <u>Preservation of Selected Works</u>. At first hand, preservation involves including a piece in the canon, considering its meaning in relation to other pieces, and allowing it to find its relative position in the whole. As we consider what may be the value of literary judgments, therefore, we have to recognize that such judgments themselves ultimately are devices of selection of a piece for inclusion in the canon. This act of inclusion enforces a tradition of literary values and attitudes that may have been in the making for years, decades, and even centuries. The judgments which make the canon possible have become more permanent than other, more fleeting assessments. This inclusion process establishes implicitly a set of literary norms. For instance, there is the classical requirement or norm that a work should foster "poetic justice," the idea that by the end of a narrative, balance between good and evil must be restored and that the so-called "good" must be seen to triumph over a putative "evil." This supposed norm, which may have been somewhat overthrown by modern narratives, enforces the notion that a work should be ethically or morally instructive – a notion to which Emerson unapologetically subscribes. By complying with this canonical suggestion, and thus by being possibly placed in the "canon," an author's work assumes a demonstrable role in the intellectual life of a culture, and the nature of this role is adjusted only by comparison with other works in the canon.

Even within the canon, some works with certain characteristics will be deemed artistically superior to others. The so-called superior works are subsequently pointed to as ideal embodiments or examples of the preferred literary qualities, and they acquire "fame" (the set of pre-formed associations and aesthetic evaluations attached to its so-called "best" authors). The canon, a kind of consummation of the process, is thus built up when works are related to and placed alongside other works similarly valued. T.S. Eliot summarizes this process of formation when he more than suggests that the cultural significance of a new work will be adjusted and readjusted with each new canonical submission.

The result is the assigning of an informal and variable rank or position to literary pieces. The canon, therefore, fixes the relative cultural position (and hence cultural value) of a work. Eliot notes that some works fluctuate in the public esteem, whereas others remain stable, preserving by and large their initial cultural positions [Eliot (46)]. This notion of placement is why Emerson had remarked earlier that to Shakespeare (whom Emerson obviously regarded as the premier genius) "they have awarded the highest place" [Emerson and Emerson (viii: 71)] or why, owing to this tendency to compare, Western audiences have made Shakespeare, after many centuries of scrutiny, by reputation "a fixed star" – "unapproachable" by other poets" [Emerson and Gilman (16: 271)].

b. Selection of New Works. At second hand, and by virtue of the relative cultural permanence it has achieved, the canon provides a potent method of selecting future works. Notoriety conferred by the canon leads new readers to take up a work, molding their tastes. Thus, the "canon" becomes a "signal" convenience [Emerson and Gilman (9: 212; 10: 368)] by saving readers time in identifying culturally designated works [Emerson and Gilman (13: 403; 16: 340)], saving them from the necessity, that is, of reading "all authors, to grope [their] way to the best." Rather, the canon provides them the luxury of choosing from the canonical or publicly-selected "best," their personal "best" [Emerson and Gilman (9: 212; 10: 368; 13: 403; 16: 340)]. By consulting with this "canon," new readers readily choose from the pieces before them those works which seem to them exceptional, within culturally-determined aesthetic limits. In doing so, the canon stimulates, provides a continuity in, or otherwise cements a relationship between previous and subsequent publics. This new audience, being nourished by the same canon, will tend to continue the tradition of adoring the same type of writers.

c. Influence of Canonical Judgments on Writers. At third hand, the canon, together with contemporary critiques, can exert an educational influence on writers themselves. But the question is, just how can this influence take place? In what way can literary judgment influence writers, and does the new writer experience

146

this influence differently from established writers? Specifically, this judgment, through its constructive (rather than destructive) influence: provides the backdrop of a largely educational experience, affecting the training of new writers and the future work of established writers.

Educational Nature of the Canonical Influence. Many writers do rebel instinctively against the for them destructive influence of canons. Their criticism may easily be that canons thwart the creativity and restrict the aesthetic freedom of new writers, impose a kind of orthodoxy, and encourage imitators rather than innovators. (Here, we have to remember Emerson's requirement that literature has to be original.) Another cogent criticism of canons is that they must become more inclusive, needing to be less ethnocentric and less gender-biased.[75]

However, we mean to focus upon the canon's intriguing constructive or educational potential. For the canon can make writers receptive to the ideas of the public, just as the public have made themselves receptive to the ideas of authors. This fact simply implies the potential for a reciprocal and mutually beneficial relationship between the two, even though, when the public sits as critic, that relationship can be strained. The unavoidably "orthodox" information from the canon is likely to solicit from authors a range of possible reactions, from abject imitation of the works in the canon to rebellion and intense disdain of them as models.

Impact Upon New Writers. Despite the "orthodoxy" which the canon implies, new writers hopefully can be, and often are,

---

[75] See Guillory, *Cultural*; "Ideology."

nurtured, by canonical models, ostensibly without limiting their artistic freedom or destroying the artistic detachment Emerson regards as needed to bring off a competent literary piece.

The canon (together with the writer's family or with critics whom new writers may encounter) provides an inevitable source from which prospective authors may develop their unique attitudes, styles, thematic views, and points of reference. The concept that a canon may be helpful or nurturing to the new writer in this way, may or may not suggest the usual manner in which we think of established tradition, which appears, again, to be of greater value in the poetic theories of a T.S. Eliot than in those of a William Wordsworth. But writers do, in fact, undergo stages of infancy and adolescence before they come into their own; and during these formative periods, a certain degree of "canonical" influence might be welcomed.

During a kind of artistic infancy, nurturing is often taken over by "fault-finding brothers and sisters at home, who will not spare" nascent writers, "but will pitch and cavil, and tell the odious truth" [Emerson and Gilman (15: 110)]. If authors are fortunate, during a succeeding (and, admittedly, theoretical) adolescent stage, they may be nurtured by a community of other writers, who prod them, taking them beyond the "grammar school" ability merely "to read and write and cipher,"[76] stopping them from forming good opinions of themselves prematurely, or of playing pranks upon an unwary public [Emerson and Gilman (8: 121 - 22)]. However, it is here that we emphasize the possible educational value of the canon, because models in the canon may also help these new writers reach a level of maturity beyond what they

---

[76] By community of writers, Emerson means "a genuine intellectual tribunal, not a literary junto of Edinburgh wits, or dull conventions of Quarterly or Gentleman's Reviews." [Emerson and Emerson (ix: 520)]

might otherwise obtain, by allowing them to study (and be influenced by) the aims, methods, and materials of widely-esteemed authors. It is true that this potential function of nurturing writers remains in its infancy; and will continue to do so (Emerson tells us) until we "unfold" the "anatomy of genius" or find "Milton in the egg" [Emerson and Gilman (9: 440)]. But the canon cannot be (nor, in fact, is it) overlooked as a useful instructional tool for those starting out.

Impact Upon Established Writers. Established writers likewise are presented with an educational opportunity; for upon the publication of a work, they cannot help noticing a phenomenon to which Paul Valery[77] has emphatically pointed. Immediately, they experience an automatic reversal in their relation to the audience. Writers move from functioning as producers of information to *recipients*, while the public comes to function as a *producer* of information. This phenomenon of functioning as a recipient is actually routine or fundamental in the experience of new writers, whose first work, being an experiment, compels them to seek the reactions of family, friends, and known fellow writers. In contrast, established writers find this reversal to be problematic. Having followed the creative process from beginning to end, they express a greater confidence in their own judgment and generally do not dwell upon what others think. When he suggests that every author (including established writers) is already in a state of unconscious receptivity by being immersed in a sea of cultural impressions that are photographic negatives waiting to be developed in a writer's very art, Marcel

---

[77] Valéry, Ambroise Paul Toussaint Jules (1871 - 1945). French poet, philosopher, and literary critic. -- For an excellent contextual study placing Valery's views within the framework of the reader-reception critique, see Cronan.

Proust[78] finds the writer's supposed independence to be at least partially illusory. Writers unconsciously rely on these impressions to construct thoughts, emotions, images, and personages that are routinely used in the concrete development of their art. Thus, even established writers act as unconscious receptors.

Admittedly, the independence upon which established writers insist, concerns, not this process of construction, but the post-publication experience. Like it or not, established writers have to decide whether to give agency to the public feedback. Believing fervently that they cannot or should not listen to their public, some will dismiss this public input out of hand. Others may do so because they believe their work is being misunderstood. Whatever the case, these unresponsive writers are likely to face some type of reckoning. The former group may be rejected because they fail to touch a nerve with the public; the latter, because their vision may be decades in advance of the sensitivities of their readers. In this latter case, writers must, as Emerson suggests, wait for an audience in succeeding generations to appreciate what they are attempting to do. This apparently occurred in the case of Thoreau's *Walden Pond*, which was a commercial failure in Thoreau's lifetime but an unassailable "classic" after his death.

Believing that listening to their public may prove valuable, responsive writers may seek answers to certain questions. They may wish to know how successful they have been in conveying their message, whether they can replicate this success, or whether they have been making mistakes or creating blunders that affect their standing with the public. If writers choose to

---

[78] Proust, Marcel or Valentin Louis Georges Eugène Marcel Proust (1871 - 1922). French novelist and critic, known especially for the novel *À la recherche du temps perdu*.

listen to the public, they are, in effect, reversing the Emersonian dictum, which now asserts that the *reader* may provide for the *writer* the overdose of that quality whereof the writer may have the underdose! This means that the writer may do well now to listen to the reader.

Those who are sensitive to such questions may use this input to benefit their art, Charles Dickens[79] being a case in point. Public response to his second novel *Oliver Twist* helped Dickens discern what degree of empathy his eponymous character had struck in his readers, and through their responses he learned that he was successful in depicting the cruelty of the British work house, the squalor of urban living, the malicious indifference of the judiciary, and the callous exploitation of children. These responses also readjusted certain racial presuppositions[80] in the early publications and stage performances of the narrative, in which Dickens grossly exploited stereotypes of the Jew in Britain. When certain readers disapproved of the portrait, he softened it, even though the final portrayal remained antisemitic. He thus participated in an implied cycle of creating an object and then of receiving feedback about this object, and this feedback must have helped to trigger his interest in creating a new piece. This audience feedback might never actually dictate how he began a new novel; but it did exert an influence. Almost certainly, powerful audience responses to his narratives helped Dickens to write novel after novel depicting different aspects of

---

[79] Dickens, Charles (1812 - 1870). Considered the greatest of the British Victorian novelists, he is the author of *Oliver Twist*, *David Copperfield*, *Tale of Two Cities* and other narrative masterpieces. His first novel, *The Pickwick Papers*, was initially published in book form in 1837.

[80] Dickens' complicated views on race, xenophobia, and imperialism are explored by Laura Peters and others, including his less than flattering depiction of Black and Native American characters.

Victorian social excesses, its class inequities, and its grotesque materialism. In doing so, these responses induced the literary creative serpent metaphorically to swallow its own tail, and through novel after novel Dickens completed old creative cycles and initiated new ones!

Thus, the public eventually forms intellectual judgments about cherished works, and these judgments can provide a system of approval of new works, stimulate the public's preservation of these works, and influence the creative future of both new and established writers. It must be emphasized that at no point are we asserting that writers must subordinate their creative energies to the canon or to contemporary critiques, for the writer must be free at every point of the creative enterprise, but we do suggest that light from the public can offer a significant educational benefit.

1. <u>**The Overarching Concerns**</u>. There are those who assert that the notion of a literary creative process, procedure, or cycle is a figment of one's imagination imposed upon a mass of unrelated and unrelatable experiences and detail. As a medical doctor once cautioned me when he asked about this project, "the patterns you think you see are simply projections or impositions of your own mind upon your data." I was taken aback by his dismissive attitude, even while I respected his medical judgment. He was implying that the discovery of a reliable or predictable process in anything having to do with the humanities was impossible and that this type of thinking must be reserved for science. But his observation belied the fundamental truth that all we come to know (including about science) is superimposed upon a variety of experiences based upon observation of demonstrable patterns. This is why Emerson's statement which I placed at the beginning of Chapter 1 is so fundamental: "Man puts things in a row/Things belong in a row/The finding of the true row is science." What I am attempting here is obviously not "science," nor could it be. But what I am exploring is a series of patterns which, much like the tenuous principles of, say, psychology, are highly suggestive and worthy of sincere consideration. Admittedly, one hindrance to the pursuit of such "patterns" has been my own background, in that I was trained in English and American language and literature. I am certain that this training carries with it many useful mental habits and productive assumptions, but I have no illusion also that this

training encompasses many biases and limiting frameworks. Nonetheless, one has to take oneself as he is.

Actually, my overarching goal was not only to throw into relief some suspected patterns, but it was also to show the many aspects of the literary creative process, not piece meal, but as a synthesis or whole. I was interested in how the perceived patterns, trajectories, aspects, arcs, or phases of a literary creative process interact or interrelate, to show the somewhat "big picture," as it may actuate itself in the mind of the writer. Behind my interest about synthesis is the far deeper one of wondering whether these or other patterns govern or must govern the working out of *any* creative idea, from mental or intuitive perception to completed form, together with any impact upon its intended audience. But this general interest could be satisfied only partially here because pursuing it presupposes thousands of projects like this one, expanded to fields outside of my own experience or competence.

2. **The Specific Assertions**. What are these perceived patterns, and how do they relate to a whole?

a. *Pre-Creative*. Emerson seems to have noted important elements of the first, preparatory, or pre-creative phase of literary production, which we have designated as vitality, commitment, and leisure. He seems to capture well the issue of vitality and is forward-thinking in bringing it up, at all. Equally refreshing are his observations about commitment. He emphasizes the need for a one-pointed mission, a determination that writers pursue their ideas, even to the point of great personal sacrifice. In certain respects, it is misleading to call the latter part of this particular discussion, "leisure," for leisure is not an end but a means. It is the nexus in which thought can occur, and it provides the doorway to the whole question of inspiration. Here, too, in this aspect of his discussion, Emerson deserves much credit for emphasizing the value of writers to society and for defending the writer's function.

b. *Creative*. Although the supposed Second or Creative Phase of literary production is more elusive than either the pre-creative or post-creative phases, useful deductions about patterns seemed possible.

Subject Matter or Inspiration. The subject matter of a piece, first of all, was shown to be the result of a dualistic process – an interaction between the presumed source, or sender, or Oversoul, and the recipient, the individualized consciousness of the writer. What is foremost in Emerson's perception is that the potential subject matter of literature is preexistent and imposed upon writers, rather than created by them. Only profound thinkers (among them writers) are capable of accessing and hence of transmitting the messages inherent in this Oversoul. Some may complain that this perception of Emerson's is aristocratic, even elitist; and such critics may point with distaste to the report that Friedrich Nietzsche[81] derived some of his notion of the Ubermensch or Superman from his reading of Emerson and from this type of Emersonian doctrine, which also informs Emerson's whole theory of history as the summation of the biographies of superior individuals. Whether this critique is fair or not, the doctrine of the gifted few remains the foundation of Emerson's creative philosophy. What is actually remarkable about this

---

[81] Nietzsche, Friedrich (1844 – 1900). Influential German philosopher, critic of Western culture, and author of *Beyond Good and Evil*.

philosophy are the Emersonian perceptions which go to explain the dynamic relationship between the Oversoul and the often-tortured writer, whose consciousness represents a prism or modifying lens. The refractions or distortions of this lens are created by writers absorbing unconsciously the assumptions of their age and culture, by their accepting the prevailing literary canon and contemporary criticisms which influence their methods and style, and by their being governed by personal traits and capabilities.

When it comes to making the desired link between the writer's consciousness and the Oversoul, the writer is left to her or his own devices. That is to say, the writer is left with the arduous task of finding, with the aid or hindrance of this individual lens, a way or ways of connecting to the Oversoul. Here, however, there is the familiar paradox, which is that there is always a method of contact which all writers will have in common because these universal methods are guides, rules, or boundaries that exist for everyone. But it is within the framework of these supposed boundaries that the *individual's* efforts come into play. The heart of the matter concerns writers' ability to arrive at moments of transcendence during which they can link their consciousness directly to the Oversoul and become a human "bridge" or channel by means of which they can ascertain or touch their ordained subject or, stated differently, by which their ordained subject can choose them as its assured vessel. We must remember Emerson's previous statement that what is needed are those who can rise to the level of the Oversoul, because they possess the mechanism, ability, or skill to do so: without this finer organization on their part, no communication with the Oversoul is possible. In the end, all of this effort may be short-circuited or destroyed, if writers lack the essential courage to follow through with what has been granted them and to implement their project with integrity, fortitude, and faith in their aim.

Growth of the Idea. Emerson makes clear that contact with the Oversoul is only the beginning of the literary cycle and that this process must enter a phase in which the topic is developed, expanded, into the literary object, for this is the only way to make any communication from the Oversoul, not only expansive enough for the writer to understand it more concretely, but also accessible to the audience for whom practically all serious writing is intended. This new phase of development seemingly demands from the writer a novel set of skills – executive ability to keep the project focused and on track; imaginative capacity which, in the writer's creative consciousness, at least, gives body to the intuitive perceptions from the Oversoul; and compositional skill, to add demonstrable form to what has been imagined but not as yet projected into a final vehicle.

Emerson opened with the notion that perceiving the truth is never enough but that writers must be endowed with certain executive skills which allow them to embody this truth – skills of focus, acquiescence to failure, and discipline. This discipline itself is expressed by Emerson through an apt analogy when he asserts that discipline is a creative way of counteracting gravity, which tends to veer writers off course, condemning them to non-achievement of their goal. But what is truly fascinating is Emerson's frank admission that literature is a clever ruse or game, devised by humans as a way of controlling that which they can never control – i.e., Nature. Literature is the creation of a secondary reality that merely mirrors Nature. At the same time, accepting this mirage that is literature allows an almost complete freedom over Nature, albeit only within the *mental* sphere. But this freedom must produce that which is new, or the creative act is valueless. And this new thing must be expressed by an unavoidable metaphorical language.

Composition. The premier requirement of compositional skill, in the final analysis, is design, which provides a positive yet flexible basis for fleshing out the object. Emerson gives a solid account of this requirement. More complicated is the issue of development. Emerson first asserts that a work must be filled with the writer's warmth, heart, or instinct because without them, the object will be to the reader lifeless. But at a deeper level, the work must also evidence the integrity or moral grounding of writers, whom we expect to be sincere if we are to grant them our time, interest, or trust. Further, the voice or style of the piece must be magnetic, able to capture the attention of the reader through a basic simplicity of expression, involving naturalness, accessibility, and engaging turn of phrase. The crowning touch, however, is the effort which must be made to render the piece truly artistic, and therefore subtle and durable. This is achieved through perspective (which keeps in mind the goal of the work), proportion (which renders the work beautiful), and selection (which adds to the work, nuances and subtleties not otherwise apparent).

Obviously, this whole discussion of the journey from perception to completed object is a difficult one, and the facts or impressions that Emerson provides might be presented in a number of ways. What stands out as uppermost, perhaps, is the realization that a chain of connections does exist that can lead to the creation of a tangible literary object on which the writer works until she or he is justified in releasing it to a public.

c. *Post-Creative*. We must begin a consideration of the post-creative phase by acknowledging again that Emerson's interest in writing always ends in the question of impact. He believed that the purpose of writing is to influence us to be and live better, and hence, writing to him is always didactic or utilitarian.

Publication. This final, or third phase of the literary creative cycle naturally presupposes publication, by means of which the work is propelled out of the sphere of the writer and into, we can say, a larger arena which necessarily implies the writer – who awaits there the public judgment. Once released, a different and derivative set of wheels takes over: the work is preserved by the public, the public ultimately makes a mental assessment of the work, and this mental assessment contributes to a literary cannon which guides aspects of the cultural future. In other words, the publication of a work starts a fertile chain reaction. It brings in the factor of the public response and sets into motion a field of interest in and of itself. By virtue of the spark which writers have built into their work, the public receives it with delight or disdain. If the book arrests the public's attention, the public preserves it and thereby extends the life of the work beyond its interaction with its creator, the author.

Audience Response. Emerson suggests that inherent in a literary piece is a three-fold magnetic thread that attracts readers differently. Some may be interested in the purely aesthetic appeal of a piece; some in its conceptual power; and others in its ethical or spiritual influence. Emerson asserts that a key magnet for the reader is the sheer beauty of a piece, because beauty itself has in it the power to elevate the public. This is the ability to make us yearn to be better than ourselves, to reach for something sublime rather than frustratingly pedestrian. At the same time, he points to the limitation that the appreciation of art for its own sake diminishes with repetition, and that the effect is most powerful when art is rarely sought for and used. A second magnet that attracts the reader is the intellectual content of the work, and in some sense, this is the most common motive for reading. This intellectual avenue offers readers the chance of comparing the components of their own mind with those of other minds and, by so doing, proffers the opportunity of revising these components. Doing so, helps the reader confront the many illusions which plague us daily, providing a platform for evaluation. It helps the reader to peer beneath the mask of illusion to discover values which are deeper and more permanent than are evident on the surface. Accordingly, the third magnet attracting a reader to a piece is the potential ability of literature to aid in the work of the seer, which is to help us discover the soul within us. In fact, for Emerson, literature which lacks an ethical center is empty and therefore worthless. And this is why he downplays the use of literature for entertainment or even for consolation.

Use of Public Judgment. In the end, the writer has started a chain of effects which reverberate through the public, not only affecting their selection and preservation of a work, but also influencing indirectly new writers or the future work of established writers. At some point, when the adoring public enters a phase in which their relationship to a work shifts from being primarily emotive to being intellectual or evaluative, a fresh area of discussion is opened up. This involves the production of fair, valid, and mature judgments about a work. But the relativity of these judgments is not necessarily a bar to their usefulness. For these judgments eventually come together to produce a literary canon which creates the incentive for the continuous selection of works, for their preservation, and for influencing new and established writers, thus completing, and at the same time possibly contributing to, the renewal of the literary creative cycle – which brings us back to the initial questions of the personal readiness of writers and later of the formation of their individual lenses, in anticipation of a new literary effort.

3. <u>Some Lingering Issues</u>. In the end, Ralph Waldo Emerson has offered us some of his isolated perceptions, not only of the personal adjustments which writers must impose upon their everyday living, not only of the more interior elements of the literary creative process, but also of the work's relation to a receptive public; and we have tried to arrange these perceptions into a coherent picture of the whole. Emerson's observations have given us but a glimpse into these issues, while at the same time leaving many questions unanswered:

a. Emerson's description of writers' responsibility towards their art presupposes a tremendous amount of personal and spiritual discipline, and hence some may complain that he sets the bar for writers unreasonably high.

b. His observations regarding the origin of literary subjects are fascinating, but the chain of causes from the Oversoul to the subject that the writer ultimately implements remains murky.

c. Emerson's equally fascinating perceptions about the workings of the creative mind that lead to the finished, refined product likewise need amplification.

d. Emerson's observations about audience selection of a published work suggest somewhat subjective patterns of public response -- patterns that, if they do exist, need to be developed far beyond the meager suggestions which Emerson offers.

e. His observations concerning the judgment of a piece evoke the perhaps premature conclusion that such judgments are unavoidably relative and that absolute principles of literary assessment are all but unattainable.

f. His perceptions regarding the possible use of these public evaluations seem to downplay the historical conflict between writer and critic, setting aside the writer's frequent (and not unfounded) complaint that literary criticism either is of no use or merely reflects the arbitrariness of the critic, thereby presenting what may seem to be an overly-idealistic picture of the potential for cooperation between writer and critic or (if one likes) between writer and audience. This impression, however, is mitigated when we consider that literary criticism, especially in the form of contemporary audience response, can be valuable to established writers, in conveying to them new information which can nurture fresh creative endeavors.

But even if many issues remain unresolved, we do acknowledge that Emerson's insights vividly open up the discussion about the mind of the writer; processes of literary creative production; and the vital interactions among the writer, the work, and the public. Given the fluid nature of the Emersonian journals, we have only indications or suggestions of these relationships; but at least we can say that Emerson has offered up some of the foundational concepts and, in so doing, has led us to an intriguing view of the big picture.

Arasteh, A R, and Josephine D. Arasteh. *Creativity in the Life-Cycle.*

   Leiden: E.J. Brill, 1968.

Cronan, Todd. "Paul Valéry's Blood Meridian, Or How the Reader

   Became a Writer." Issue No. 1. January 25, 2011. *Nonsite.org.*

   nonsite.org/article/paul-valery-from-author-to-audience.

Eliot, Thomas Stearns. *The Sacred Wood: Essays on Poetry and*

   Criticism. Avenel Press, 2017.

_____. "What Is Minor Poetry?" *On Poetry and*

   Poets (New York: Farrar, Straus and Company, 1943; rpt.

   1957): 46.

Emerson, Ralph Waldo, and Edward W. Emerson. *Journals of Ralph*

   Waldo Emerson with Annotations. 1911 ed., Vols. 10,

   Houghton Mifflin, 1909.

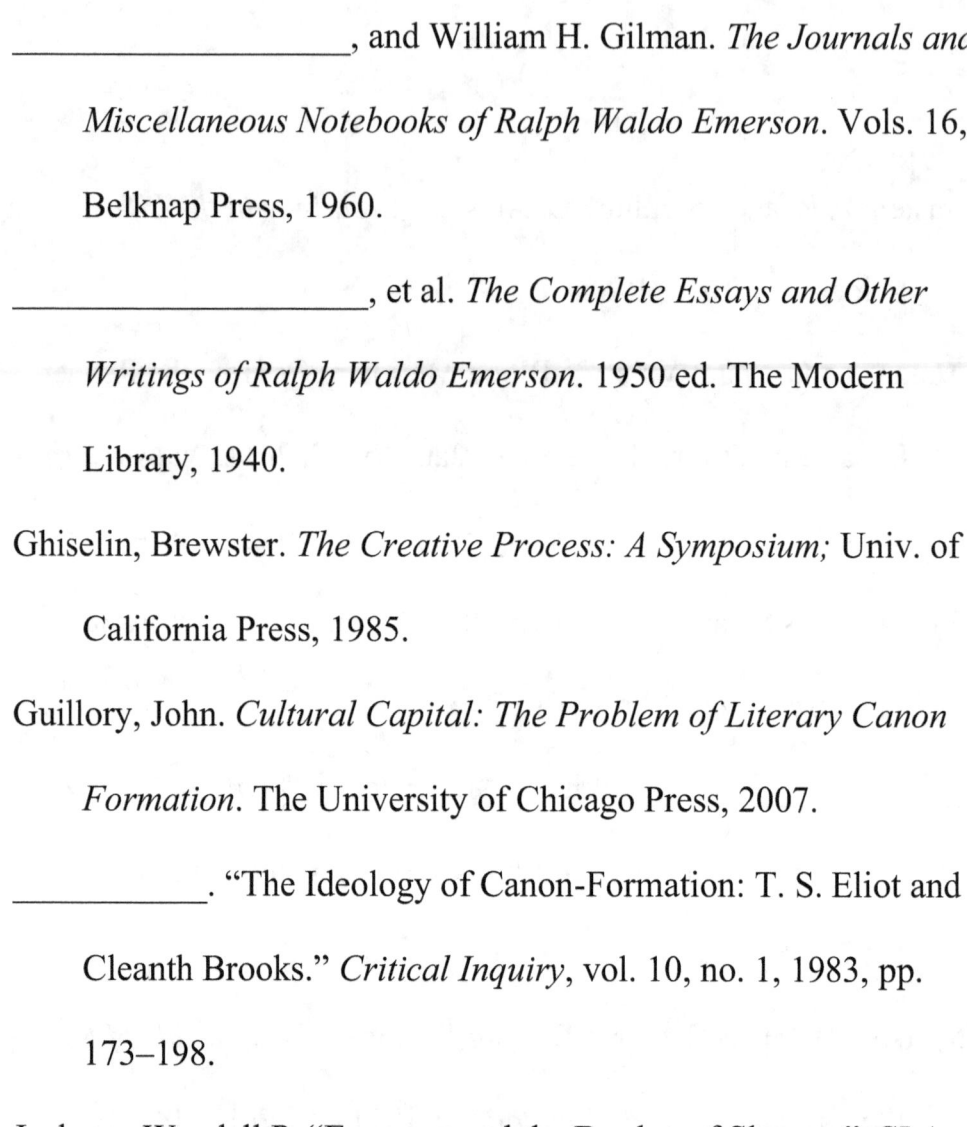

_____, and William H. Gilman. *The Journals and Miscellaneous Notebooks of Ralph Waldo Emerson*. Vols. 16, Belknap Press, 1960.

_____, et al. *The Complete Essays and Other Writings of Ralph Waldo Emerson*. 1950 ed. The Modern Library, 1940.

Ghiselin, Brewster. *The Creative Process: A Symposium;* Univ. of California Press, 1985.

Guillory, John. *Cultural Capital: The Problem of Literary Canon Formation*. The University of Chicago Press, 2007.

_____. "The Ideology of Canon-Formation: T. S. Eliot and Cleanth Brooks." *Critical Inquiry*, vol. 10, no. 1, 1983, pp. 173–198.

Jackson, Wendell P. "Emerson and the Burden of Slavery." *CLA Journal* 25, no. 1 (September 1981), 55.

_____. "Theory of the Creative Process in the 'Prefaces' of Henry James." *Amid Visions and Revisions: Poetry and Criticism on Literature and the Arts*. Ed. Burney J. Hollis. Baltimore: Morgan State University Press, 1985. 59-64.

James, Henry. *The Novels and Tales of Henry James*, Vol. 7. New York Edition (New York: Charles Scribner's Sons, 1908): xxi.

Kant, Immanuel. Critique of Judgment. A & D Publishing, 2018.

Peters, Laura. *Dickens and Race*. Manchester University Press, 2013.

Plimpton, George, and Joyce Carol Oates. *Writers at Work: the Paris Review Interviews*. Penguin, 1990.

Rothenberg, Albert. *The Creativity Question*. Duke Univ. Press, 1996.

Sartre, Jean-Paul. *"What Is Literature?" and Other Essays*. Harvard University Press, 1988.

Schoen, Max, and Jacques Maritain. "Creative Intuition in Art and

Poetry." *College Art Journal*, vol. 13, no. 2, 1954, p. 148.

Spencer, Herbert. *The Principles of Sociology by Herbert Spencer*.

Vol. 1, Williams and Norgate, 15, Henrietta Street, Covent

Garden, London, 1876.

Wellek René, and Austin Warren. *Theory of Literature*. Harcourt

Brace & Company, 1994.

Wordsworth, William, et al. *Lyrical Ballads*. Pearson Longman,

2007.

World Literature Today, vol. 67, no. 2, 1993, p. 460.

Wendell Jackson received his B.A. degree in English from Loyola College in Maryland and his M.A. and Ph.D. degrees in English and American Language and Literature from Harvard University. He also was the recipient of the Woodrow Wilson, Fulbright, and Danforth Foundation Fellowships. He taught college English at Morgan State University for nearly 40 years. He has written on the humanities, literary creative theory, Ralph Waldo Emerson, and Charles W. Chesnutt, and he has thought about the current topic for many years.

Index